BIOISM: The Deity of Life

By
Gary Wilson

BIOISM: The Deity of Life

By Gary Wilson

Second Edition

www.garywilson.ca

ISBN-13: 978-0-9920628-3-5

Table of Contents

FOREWORD

Truth: Embrace its seekers; beware its sellers.

Caveat lector!

GARY WILSON

THE AGE OF SOPHISTRY

Though all are born philosophers, few remain so. Philosophy, Philosophy, wherefore art thou, Philosophy?

Is it me? – my imagination? Am I jaded? Or is there a dearth of philosophy today? Knowledge, good knowledge, real knowledge, certainly is not lacking. Nor is the love of it. Philognosy – if I may invent a word – is alive and kicking. We are swimming in a vast ocean of knowledge, perhaps even drowning in knowledge. Yet, where is wisdom? Knowledge, knowledge, everywhere; but where is wisdom? Where is philosophy?

After two and a half millennia of philosophy, the greatest philosopher of all remains Socrates, the progenitor of the breed, a stonemason who penned not a single word for posterity. Who is there nowadays that compares to him? Nobody. Nobody! Him, one simple stonemason, versus us in our sophistication and our billions, scientists, engineers, doctors, mathematicians, theologians, not to mention stonemasons and carpenters too. All we seem to manage, all I seem to see in looking around, is sophistry, a uniform horizon of sophistry.

The problem with philosophy in the modern age is not with the state of human knowledge, nor with that of human intelligence – both of which are more advanced now than ever before, nor even with that of human virtue, the disappearance or degradation of which is mourned anew unceasingly by each succeeding generation. No, the problem with philosophy today stems from none of these things. The problem with philosophy stems from the vastness of the field human knowledge has revealed to us. The philosopher, the true philosopher, is a general who must survey this whole field; he is an Alexander who must acquaint himself with his theatre of war in its entirety. The problem with philosophy today is that whereas we need generals, we have only champions; whereas we need strategy, we are offered only tactics; whereas we need an Arthur, we are given instead a brigade, a division, an army, of Lancelots. The problem with philosophy today is with the philosophers of today, men blinded to the forest by the trees, daunted by the vastness of the field, drowning in the ocean where they swim. The problem with philosophy today is that the generalists have surrendered to the specialists.

Is it any wonder that superstition is once again rearing its ugly head? – that this Hydra is rearing its multitude of heads, old and new? Don't blame the specialists – the physicists with their wave-particles, the astronomers with their multiverses, the psychologists with their envies, to name but a few – who view reality through the narrow lenses of their own disciplines. A gravitation toward the outré is all too easy (too pride-reassuring, really) whenever expert knowledge reaches a plateau in comprehension, an obstacle to progress, a moment of inadequacy. Don't blame the specialists! Blame the generalists! Blame the philosophers! Blame philosophy! For philosophy is our bulwark against superstition, against both superstition and the sophistry that feeds and nourishes it.

GARY WILSON

INTRODUCTION TO BIOISM

[The following document, originally titled 'ALTERNATIVE TWO: 'BIOCENTRISM' – DOCTORAL DISSERTATION PROPOSAL – PHILOSOPHY' serves well as an introduction to bioism.]

CONTEXT

Humanism is the dominant thought system in the world today. It has entirely overwhelmed all others. This has been accomplished through the consistent demonstration of the superiority of its logic over that of competing systems. However, humanism is not without its flaws, the most glaring of which has come clearly into view only in the past few decades. This primary flaw is at the very heart of humanism: it is its focus, its orientation, the fact that such orientation is centered on humanity, exclusively on humanity.

OVERVIEW

"Bioism" is what I call my model of reality, a new and, I believe, creative contribution to the field of philosophy; it is the daughter of humanism, borrowing the bulk of its logic and differing mainly in the matter of focus. Whereas humanism sees everything revolving around humanity, bioism sees everything revolving around life in general. Humanity may represent the most complex life form and therefore may be the flagship of life, yet it is still only a part of the system, and not the system itself. No matter how special and unique we are or see ourselves to be, humanity is not an island divorced from the rest of life. We are, and must conduct ourselves, not apart from, but as a part of, this system, of life in general.

This focus on life in general is the primary differentiating aspect of bioism. Simple though it may sound, it has major ramifications. Gone is morality based on human whim and fancy; in its place is one that studies biology, including the human, and develops its precepts in light of the whole system rather than merely the mind of man. Gone are the political dogmas of humanism (its clay feet, really); in their place are reasoned arguments leading to the same protections such dogmas sought to provide. Gone is technological progress at any and all costs; in its place is sustainable development implemented after evaluation of both its utility and systemic effects. And gone is the take-no-prisoners approach to metaphysics; in its place is a more properly agnostic, even if skeptical, stance of toleration toward those pursuing life on a plane other than the physical. These are just a few examples of the impact of this shift in focus from humanity to life in general.

BIOISM: THE DEITY OF LIFE

'Bioism' is also the title of the collection of twenty-one essays expounding this philosophy of the same name. Seven of these essays are entirely peripheral, pure application. Of the remaining fourteen, four are core and one, 'Biosity', is the wellspring of all but the prefatory essays. These writings have been composed over a period of six years, some gestating for months and years prior to their ultimate appearance (one even taking fully six years). The following is a list of them along with a basic flowchart showing their relationship to each other:

1. THE AGE OF SOPHISTRY (9/03) - 550 words
2. MODELS OF REALITY (6/03) - 1450 words
3. BIOSITY (11/97) - 6100 words
4. THE TENTH POINT OF METABIOSITY (4/01) - 50 words
5. BIOFEROSITY: THE NEW STANDARD OF MORALITY (2/01) - 1250 words
6. CONTROL (3/01) - 2000 words
7. DEMOCRACY: WILL IS THE ESSENCE OF LIFE (4/02) - 2150 words
8. OUTLINE OF GOVERNMENT (12/02) - 2700 words
9. MONOCULTURE, MONOCULT (2/03) - 1250 words
10. SEX CLINTON-STYLE (7/03) - 900 words
11. THE MOTHERLESS SOCIETY (5/03) - 2350 words
12. ESCAPISM (8/03) - 3800 words
13. RITUAL AND TABOO

14. MEANS (4/03) - 550 words
15. ATOMIC ROTATIONAL SPEED EXPERIMENT (6/03) - 350 words
16. METABIOSITY (4/01) - 900 words
17. MISCELLANEOUS OBSERVATIONS ON JUSTICE (12/02) - 900 words
18. COSMOPOLESE (7/03) - 6650 words
19. PROPOSAL: METRICIZED TIME (AND ANGLE) MEASUREMENT (1/98) - 900 words
20. LEAPWEEK: A CALENDAR REFORM PROPOSAL (4/03) - 900 words
21. YEAR DESIGNATION (8/03) - 1000 words

[FLOW CHART REMOVED.]

PROCEDURE

My position on philosophy is that, of all disciplines, it is the least amenable to specialization. The genuine philosopher is a generalist, and genuine philosophy is accessible to everyone. Therefore, the setting down of a philosophy is a task that requires, in place of a formally scholastic approach, a lifestyle of research, observation, investigation and analysis; and the procedure to be followed calls for ninety-eight parts thought, one part writing and one part revision.

BIOISM: THE DEITY OF LIFE

Beginning in late 1996 the first threads of bioism began to coalesce and grow in my mind. I wrote nothing down then. At the time I was avoiding an arrest warrant, thus traveling constantly and experiencing a kaleidoscope of lifestyles. In May 1997 I turned myself in and began a wait, under detention, of over four years before reaching trial. This detention was not conducive for much, but it was conducive for pondering and, at times, writing philosophy, so that only a few months after my surrender I composed 'Biosity', the heart of bioism. This one essay alone represents many hundreds of hours of thought and its composition proceeded at a pace averaging little more than a page per day. Apart from work, mostly preliminary, on a few minor essays, it was three years of continued contemplation until I began to compose the other major essays further elucidating the thought contained in 'Biosity'. In late 2001 my court proceedings were complete and my incarceration in prison began. After a couple more essays over the next year I took stock of all that I had written up till then as well as the notes I had outlining subsequent writings. I determined what was necessary to fill various gaps in the exposition of bioism and I tackled each of these essays as the muse directed me. A couple additional essays came out of nowhere – of course, there is nowhere that is nowhere in the mind – and forced themselves on me, so I relented and gave them their due as well. It is now fall 2003 and I have just completed, over the last few weeks, an overall revision encompassing all of the essays in 'Bioism' (with the exception of 'Ritual and Taboo', which I have not yet written). Of particular interest I would like to note that 'Biosity', the first and founding essay, required nothing beyond some substitution of revised terms and two revisions in one short section; which is to say that throughout a period of almost six years representing a minimum of six thousand hours of contemplation and composition, my thought, my new model of reality, has remained stable.

The above description represents that part of the procedure I have already undertaken. Normally, study accomplished prior to formally entering a doctoral program would be excluded from application toward the requirements of that program. I can only hope that an examination of my circumstances over the last six years due to incarceration – confinement, varying mail restrictions, denial of Internet access, phone access limited (here) to twenty minutes per year, total lack of income, the institutional denial of a local professor's kind offer to mentor me onsite in a graduate program – will result in the acceptance of my scholarly effort throughout this time as an applicable element of my doctoral studies. I am not asking for any relaxation of scholastic standards; rather, I wish to demonstrate that, in spite of serious disadvantages, my undertakings as a scholar here are valid, even if unconventional.

The next stage of the procedure (assuming the completion of 'Ritual and Taboo') involves the submission of 'Bioism' to a trio of critics. This will not be simply the provision of manuscripts with a request for review and comments. Rather, the essays will be submitted one by one, first to last over a period of a year or two. For each essay the critics will first be asked to read it thoroughly and write down their questions and comments; they will do this independently of each other. A few days thereafter all four of us will meet in a casual setting for a two- to four-hour session to discuss the essay; I will be recording and transcribing these conversations. The purpose of such discussion will be to evaluate the structural integrity of bioism and the degree of validity it represents. It will be my aim to respond fully to all the written questions and comments, whether such involves clarification, explanation, commentary, or even revision on my part. However, these sessions will not have any rigid structure to them; answers often breed further questions and the format will be free discourse. It goes without saying that this process cannot commence until I have regained my freedom. Once it has commenced we will witness a growing body of material – eventually quite immense – that, when complete, will complement 'Bioism' so that the two together, 'Bioism' itself (possibly in revised form at that point) and our collected discourses on it, will represent the totality of the studies to be performed and submitted by myself as part of this doctoral program. My intent, in proposing this discourse method, is to

13

substitute the product of it for the conventional research normally required in doctoral studies, something which not only am I unable to provide in these circumstances but also I maintain would be neither suitable nor feasible in the development of a work so unspecialized and holistic as a philosophy.

QUALIFICATIONS

My qualifications for this include:

1. BA in History, University of Calgary, June 1989

2. Certificate in Safety and Environmental Studies, Southern Alberta Institute of Technology, September 1995, including:
   a. Developing Codes of Practice
   b. Risk Assessment
   c. Incident Investigation
   d. Root Cause Analysis

3. 97 percentile ranking, Law School Admissions Test, June 1995. The LSAT is essentially a series of difficult puzzles to be solved; philosophy too can be approached as a series of difficult puzzles to be solved.

4. Broad life experience, including numerous jobs and businesses, foreign culture immersion, a fair bit of travel, far more adventure than necessary, intimate exposure to the workings of the legal system as well as to a myriad of lifestyles and perspectives, licit or otherwise, and most of all, constant and thoughtful analysis of every passing thing that has seemed significant.

5. Further life experience vicariously gained through reading (mostly) or otherwise accessing the thoughts and ideas of others, whether such be overtly philosophical or inherently so, as in the case of art, or of literature.

GARY WILSON

MODELS OF REALITY

Space, time and matter together form reality. Space and time are analog, whereas matter is digital, or more precisely, binary. To put this another way, matter differs from space and time in that it is always either "is" or "is-not". In contrast, space is always "is-not", and time is always "is". The relationship of time to space is not simply that of a fourth dimension to the three more familiar ones. Time is dimensional in that it behaves mono-dimensionally, and for the purpose of perception it is useful to see and interpret time as a line, a single dimension with a "before" section and an "after" section separated by the present, that point on the line we call "now". However, useful though this construction may be, the fact is that time is not the line, but rather merely the point on the line; therefore time, in reality, is not a dimension, but instead an element of a dimension, with the further limitation that its movement within this single dimension is both uniform (of unchanging speed) and progressive (unidirectional, anisotropic). What it is that gives us the impression that time is a dimension, rather than merely a point in a dimension (the "temporal" dimension), is inertia, an aspect not of time or space, but of matter. Because we see processes, which are inherently forms of inertia interacting among themselves, as being lines with starting-points and finishing-points along that

17

dimension in which time exists as a point, we analogously extrapolate time itself to be a line rather than the mere point on a line it actually is. Look at the inertia of a baseball (setting aside the complex of inertias and considering only the ball's movement in one spatial dimension): The pitcher throws the ball and half a second later the catcher catches it. We see this holistically within the context of an overall process that takes a half second to transpire, and therefore we assume that a half second exists as such. Reality "sees" the same, not holistically from start to finish, but rather as an ongoing "snapshot in time" (the only "perspective" available under the tyranny of time) in which, at any given point of observation, the baseball has one single precise position in its spatial dimension (rather than a movement per se) along with whatever inertia will contribute to any future change in this position. Whereas space, in all its three-dimensionality, is fully interactive, time is relentlessly non-interactive. There is no such thing in reality as the past, nor of the future; these are merely abstractions, one a recollection, the other an extrapolation. Reality knows only what exists. Time's complete substance is realized and contained in the infinitesimally small – and infinitely broad – point that is the present.

Space is three-dimensional, yet absent matter it is a void of indeterminate dimension. Matter is needed for the observation and measurement of space's dimensions, and such measurement is contextualized entirely by matter: matter on matter demonstrating space. Similarly, the observation and measurement of the progression of time is dependent entirely on matter.

We perceive abstractions as strictly insubstantial, as immaterialities however influential they may be. In reality, though, abstractions have substance. A thought in my head is not simply the representation of an external reality or realities; it is, in and of itself, a reality, a material arrangement of neurons or molecules in a pattern that is recognizable to and accessible by my cognition. I am unable to deliver this material thing to anyone else because its existence is such that I alone have access to it. Nevertheless, I can create a second material thing reflective of this first material thing, the thought in my head, that I can then deliver to others if I have put it into a form accessible to them. That second material thing may be a writing, the arrangement of ink deposits on the surface of a bleached wood pulp membrane; or an utterance, the creation of sound waves using air as the medium and presumably within range of a listener or storage device; or a gesture, a meaningful body movement performed presumably in the sight of a viewer and using reflected photons as the medium; or an embrace, a bodily motion conducting meaning between two persons using no intervening medium beyond their own tactile sense; or an e-mail, with its eight or so stages of intervening media between the originating mind and the receiving mind; or an art object such as a statue, a physical substance formed so as to be viewed or even felt by others; not to mention innumerable other forms of expression along with their endless permutations. In all cases, the end result of a successful such transmission is the creation in the receiver's mind of a material arrangement of neurons or molecules in a pattern that is recognizable to and accessible by his cognition and approximates in some meaningful way the parent pattern contained in the originator's mind.

Abstractions are models of reality. The term "model", in this context, can be taken in either of two senses: as a representation, or as an example. In the case of abstractions both senses are applicable. The regular perception of abstractions is that they are representations of reality – and this is correct, but we have just seen that they are also examples of reality in and of themselves. An abstraction being transmitted from one mind to a second mind is a model of reality (in both senses), and in each intermediate stage it becomes a new model of reality (again, in both senses). A very different situation is when an abstraction is the inspiration of an action which is not inherently a form of expression: in this case the resulting model of reality is a model only in the single sense of being an example. For instance, when a boy imagines a paper airplane, he has created in his mind a model of reality which is both an example and a representation of reality; then when he draws his idea on paper he has created a new model of reality, still both a representation and an example of reality; but when he actually folds the paper into an airplane, assuming that his only purpose in such creation is the pleasure of flying the toy, the resulting model of reality – the airplane – is no longer a representation of reality, but only an example.

It becomes apparent what an immensely broad concept is covered by the term "model of reality", as broad as that of "thing". A photon is a model of reality. The sun is a model of reality. A person. A lifestyle. An activity. An occupation. A belief. A perspective. A tool. A possession. A dollar bill. A home. A business. A roof. A floor. A beam. A stone. An ant. An ant colony. A book. A play. A movie. All of these are models of reality in the sense that they are examples of reality, and some in the additional sense that they are representations of it.

Let us now narrow our focus to those models of reality which represent reality. A man may make the study of prehistoric snails, for instance, the central effort of his life, and in so immersing himself he may find the subject quite engaging. If he is an effective communicator, his enthusiasm and interest will tend to infect others to some degree. However, of far greater significance, to both the scholar himself and his audience, than the knowledge gleaned of the lives of snails (in this case) is the enlightenment gained by subsequently applying such knowledge to an understanding of any aspect of life and reality in general. It is their significance to our understanding of reality that can make even the most foreign and obscure models of reality fascinating. The value, therefore, of such a representational model of reality is proportional in one dimension to the fidelity of its adherence to and subsequent depiction of reality, and in another to the breadth of reality it addresses.

Our goal as intelligent beings, a goal toward which we have made great strides in the past few centuries, is to develop a representational model of reality that is both accurate and comprehensive; a representational model of reality that unites and reconciles all the disparate and competing models into a single, over-arching network of enlightenment; a representational model of reality that is for all means and purposes reality itself.

BIOSITY

THE FIFTH FORCE

Science has discovered four forces in the universe: gravity, electro-magnetism, the strong nuclear force and the weak nuclear force. Which of these four drives this pen as I write? Is it gravity? No. While the pen's proper functioning may require gravity, this force in and of itself does not move the pen. Electromagnetism? No. The nuclear forces? Again, no. The pen's existence may depend on these forces, but they do not drive it. The movement of this pen is not driven by any of the four forces discovered to date by science, whether singly or in combination. Therefore, either this pen is not moving, or it is, and is driven by a force other than the four identified by science. In fact there is a fifth force in the universe, and for it I have coined the term "biosity". This word means "life"; however, it has a much narrower definition than does the word "life", and refers to life in the strictly physical, scientific sense of an identifiable force in the universe, a force as separate from the other four as they are from each other.

Just as Newton observed gravity in the fall of an apple, so I observe biosity in my hand's movement of this pen, or the growth of an apple tree, or the ripening of an apple till it drops, or the rotting of that same apple. With certain sterile exceptions, such as the heart of the Sahara or portions of Antarctica, biosity is present and can be observed everywhere on Earth, whether on land or on sea. And perhaps someday we shall be able to determine whether biosity is localized to our planet alone or is widespread throughout the universe.

THE NATURE OF BIOSITY

The nature of biosity is imprinted on every single biositic entity, from plankton to redwoods, from the amoeba to the blue whale, and is thus manifest to science, individually, collectively and systemically. To study a rose, a pack of wolves or a rainforest is to study biosity.

All biositic entities have two fundamental objectives: the maintenance of being, and the exertion of will. Survival and procreation are the two efforts undertaken in the maintenance of being. The exertion of will is actualized in the control and use of space and matter, whether that be territory, material objects or other biositic entities; and it dictates that biosity is innately expansive. The biositic cycle (birth, life, reproduction and death of individual entities) is an important tool in the expansion of biosity, and provides the means for the incremental functioning which is the basis of evolution.

At one time on Earth there was but one simple organism, the first appearance of biosity here. How did this organism appear? Who can say? Perhaps there is something inherent in the elements which in certain precise conditions fosters the generation of biosity. Why is there gravity? Or electro-magnetism? Where did the atom come from? Who can really comprehend infinity, or eternity? There are some things which in ways are currently beyond the ken of science, things we acknowledge as natural in spite of their attendant mysteries.

This first organism found its niche and lived there. It reproduced and eventually died. The offspring of this organism had offspring, and so the cycle went. Through untold generations these offspring adapted so as to exploit most perfectly the niche in which they lived. And simultaneously, various branches of the offspring discovered different niches, and each of these branches adapted bit by bit to their own niches. The imprint of biosity drove these organisms to expand their territories, both by filling their niches and discovering new niches. This process has continued to the present day, and has resulted in an amazing diversity of biositic entities, most of which not only fill niches but create them as well. And this diversity, along with the adaptability provided by the biositic cycle, has so far allowed biosity to withstand the tremendous stresses brought about by environmental change.

So, what is the nature of biosity? Being, thus will. Will, thus being. There is no separating the two: will and being, being and will. Volo, ergo sum. I will, therefore I am. No being, no entity, is without will. No will is without being. The nature of biosity is will – being and will. As to the various aspects flowing from such nature, biosity is, first and foremost, expansive; it seeks to expand the territory in which it can exist, and its utilization and control of that territory. The other aspects of biosity contribute toward its expansiveness: it is cycle-oriented; it is diversifying; and it is resilient. Biosity is many other things, but these aspects represent the basis. To study and comprehend biosity best we must study nature, as opposed to mankind, because sapience has made humanity a very difficult and confusing study in biosity.

A SPECULATION ON CANCER

Here in the late twentieth century, cancer seems to be the greatest curse. We spend billions of dollars researching and combating it. We assault our persons with toxic chemicals, radiation and devastating surgical operations in our fight against it. And what are we fighting? Our very own bodies; our very own living healthy cells growing healthily in our bodies. The only problem with these living, healthy cells growing healthily is that the growth they are forming is an abnormality and threatens the health of the organism as a whole. Cancer is misdirected healthy growth, and therefore we view it as a disease.

This normal perception of cancer, as being a disease, may be erroneous. It is possible that we are missing something here, and this oversight is responsible for our error. Perhaps cancer, rather than being a disease, is the result of a normal biositic function of every organism. This interpretation, strange as it initially sounds, seems to fit the facts: The theory of evolution is generally accepted today; nevertheless, that theory is not without its problems. The main area of difficulty we have with evolution centers around mutation as being the vehicle of change. The contention that random mutation has resulted in the evolution of homo sapiens is very problematic. For one thing, a general rule of mutation is that a mutant organism is less viable than his unmutated counterparts. And for another, the number of mutations, each accounted for by at least one generation, just for the evolution, increment by increment, of man from monkey is absolutely enormous and compounded geometrically by the contention that such mutations were random, implying as that does that for every successful step forward there was a great number of missteps. However, these difficulties are overcome if there is imprinted on every organism a biositic such mechanism – a mutation function (mutation/evolution function).

Is the idea of a mutation function so very outlandish? If you were to embark on a serious weight-lifting program, what would you observe after a few months? You would observe that your muscles had grown larger and stronger. Or if you were to fall and scrape your elbow, what would you see happening over the following few days? You would see the scrape scab over and then heal with new skin, scar tissue. Our bodies respond, without conscious effort, to various stimuli, and adjust themselves accordingly. If our bodies are able to do this, to determine the need for, and to make, various adjustments, large and small, all without even our slightest conscious thought, is it not perfectly conceivable that in the same way they are able to recognize desirable structural changes (which they are not able to enact upon themselves) and program such changes into the genes that they pass on in the reproductive process? If this mutation function exists, then it is likely inherently conservative. Perhaps it is very incremental, allowing only minor change per increment. Or perhaps it has some sort of evaluation mechanism, such as allowing a change to occur only after it has been programmed into the genes of twenty successive generations. There are many possibilities.

Returning to the topic of cancer, this perspective answers a couple very important questions: Why is cancer so widespread today? Because in the last century mankind has drastically altered the planet. Throughout most of our history, human progress has had no real impact on the environment. With a few exceptions such as the refinement of metals, and the production and distillation of alcohol, we humans have generally conducted ourselves, and our progress, within our environment much as the animals do. However, this began to change in the nineteenth century as the population rose and knowledge expanded. But it was in the twentieth century that the explosive growth in the environmentally-sensitive industries occurred, those industries which produce, as product or by-product, unnatural phenomena or substances, whether synthetic or merely refined – a few examples being the nuclear, petrochemical, processed food and pharmaceutical industries. Suddenly the mutation function, which normally deals with incremental change in a fundamentally stable environment, is hit with literally hundreds of new factors, many of which are drastically novel. Is it any wonder that in so many cases it gets overloaded and malfunctions, thereby producing cancers? The only surprise is that so many of us are not afflicted. Look at diet alone: How many unnatural substances would you find if you made a list of the ingredients for everything you consumed in just one week? Ten? Fifty? A hundred or more? And that is just what you ingest. Add what you inhale and touch, even what you view and hear. If the suggested mutation function does exist, do we not give it every reason to malfunction and go berserk?

The other primary question regarding cancer is, of course, how do we get rid of it? If the previous reasoning is correct, then the surest approach is to remove the factors which potentially lead to its development. But that could be a lot of factors. Look around you. What is natural? Maybe some wood (covered in stain and varnish)? Certain fabrics (bleached and dyed)? What is synthetic or refined? Almost everything: plastics, metals, paints, fabrics, glass, concrete, asphalt, foods, soaps and fuels, to name just a few things. How realistic is it to suggest adopting a lifestyle like that of the Amish? Not very. However, perhaps a somewhat realistic program could be suggested. Perhaps, like the fight against pollution, the first ninety per cent of this problem can be overcome with a relatively minimal effort. The most obvious area for change is food, since after ingesting it we break it down and spread it throughout our entire systems. If we were to revert completely to unprocessed foods, thereby accepting a blander diet and certain inconveniences regarding storage and preparation, we would likely, in one fell swoop, attain the desired ninety per cent (assuming the unprocessed foodstuffs themselves were untainted by unwanted substances, such as steroids, antibiotics and pesticides). Another prime target is household chemicals, everything from fragrances and make-up items to paints and cleaners; again, changes here would involve certain inconveniences, and would also likely necessitate adjustments in tolerance levels vis-à-vis vanity (or personal presentation), but would at the same time be very worthwhile. In these two areas, foods and household chemicals, the individual exercising a degree of self-denial has the ability to avoid scores upon scores of unnatural substances, factors which potentially contribute to the development of cancer. Larger issues, such as industrial pollution, nuclear power generation and the development and production of synthetic substances, are in the hands of business, society and government, and will hopefully be dealt with in the future with more caution and less heedless enthusiasm than in the past. But leaving those aside, with a bit of determination by each of us individually, we can likely reduce the incidence of cancer by a great extent. This is all assuming that the suggested mutation function does in fact exist and work somewhat as described.

HOMO SAPIENS AND SAPIENCE

Sapience sets humanity apart within the crush of biosity on Earth. We are unlike any other animal, and unlike plants or other organisms. They are natural; we are not. Sapience has made us otherworldly, and worldly too. It has opened our eyes, yet we are blind, it so often seems.

Animals are "biocentrics". A "biocentric" is an organism that conducts itself as an exemplification of biosity. Humans aside, this term applies to all biositic entities (disregarding the manmade distortion of domesticated flora and fauna). In studying humans we must introduce two more terms: "metaphysicist" and "sensophreniac". A "metaphysicist" is someone who seeks to discover life on a plane other than the physical; such a person is responding to a biositic urge, but in an unnatural way. A "sensophreniac" is someone whose focus is on physical sensation. There are two types of sensophreniac: the active and the passive. An active sensophreniac is a seeker of pleasure and may be gratified by aural, visual, tactile, gastronomic, hallucinogenic, sensual, chemical or even aromatic means. A passive sensophreniac is an avoider of discomfort, whether that comes in the form of fear, pain, fatigue or merely unpleasant physical sensation. The sensophreniac too is responding to biositic urges; however, the focus of the sensophreniac is so narrow that his conduct cannot be described as exemplifying biosity, not holistically so. Where the biocentric is sensor-informed, the sensophreniac is sensor-driven.

Few, if any, among us represent a pure form of the biocentric, the metaphysicist or the sensophreniac. Our belief structures, whether religions, philosophies or unsystematized personal codes, generally reflect a mixture of the three; and where a religion or philosophy does not reflect a mixed form, its application normally does, particularly after the first burst of enthusiasm.

All religions, by definition, have a metaphysical focus. But how many are not biocentric as well? In Judaism and Christianity God admonishes Man to 'be fruitful and multiply and fill the earth.' In polytheistic religions one of the primary gods is generally a fertility deity. And in pantheistic and animistic practice fertility rites are fundamental. But such obvious details aside, religion is biocentric because it is a vehicle for introducing order into societies; and ordered societies can expand more successfully than can unordered societies. Religion can also be sensophrenic, or exhibit sensophrenic tendencies in practice (particularly to the benefit of the hierarchy), but this is less constant and pervasive. One example of a religion with an overt sensophrenic component is Tantric Buddhism. So religion is metaphysical, usually biocentric and often sensophrenic to some degree as well. (The only good examples that come to mind of religionists with a purely metaphysical focus are the hermit monks of early Christianity and the suicide cultists that occasionally appear today. The hermits severely limited their territories (often to a small cell or even the top of a pole), rejected procreation and gloried in discomfort and abnegation; they all but preceded the cultists in suicide, the ultimate test of faith in a metaphysical realm, and likely would have done that too but for the teachings of the Church.)

Followers of philosophies or personal codes, on the other hand, are not generally perceived to have a metaphysical focus; yet they too are hard-pressed to set metaphysics entirely aside. There are many fundamental concepts common to much philosophical thought which must be accepted either as predicated on metaphysical bases or as the dogmas, the untenable, quasi-metaphysical dogmas, which they are. Let's look at just a couple examples: equality and morality. The concept of equality is central to humanism, democracy, the rule of law, socialism, feminism and progressivism. Metaphysicists have a rational basis for accepting this concept if they maintain that God, or whatever higher authority than ourselves, values each and every human being equally. But non-metaphysicists, having no such authority mechanism, must predicate equality on the fact of our common biological status; yet, equality and similarity are not the same thing, and a position which must assume that they are will ultimately prove to be untenable. However, the non-metaphysicist who perceives equality as a useful concept for the structuring of human society, rather than as an unquestioned and eternal dogma at the heart of his philosophy, is on very solid ground; but non-metaphysicists with such a perspective are very rare since the position of the quasi-metaphysical dogma is so much more satisfying and definite.

Our other example, the concept of morality, is similar in many ways to what we have just seen regarding equality: It is central to many philosophies, doctrines and practices. Employing an authority mechanism such as God, the metaphysicists have a rational basis for it. And there is a good, non-metaphysical basis for morality if it is perceived merely as a useful concept for ordering society, rather than as an unquestioned dogma; nevertheless, the vast majority of non-metaphysicists prefers the security of a definite position and therefore clings to various quasi-metaphysical bases for morality, one good example being "natural law."

This expanded perspective, perceiving human thought and action as exhibiting biocentric, metaphysical and/or sensophrenic traits, in contrast to the pure bioism of non-human biositic entities (setting aside the domesticated), is an important tool in comprehending homo sapiens. With it we can look at any philosophy, attitude, teaching, practice or activity and discover just what blend of the three components it is. This is crucial because we as humans have discarded instinct, our innate guidance mechanism, in favor of conscious thought, which is dependent on accurate observation and reasoning. We must understand our thoughts and deeds so that we can judge them well; and ultimately, the only proper standard against which we should measure such judgment is biosity. That which fosters biosity, or facilitates biositic goals, is "bioferous", life-bearing; whereas that which hinders, retards, attacks or destroys biosity is "necroferous", death-bearing.

THE PRINCIPLES OF BIOSITY APPLIED TO MANKIND

We have looked at the nature of biosity as seen in the natural world, and we have contrasted the biocentric, metaphysical and sensophrenic aspects of humanity with the simple bioism of the rest of biosity. The question we must now confront is this: Is the divergence of mankind from the norms of biosity bioferous or necroferous? This is a very large and complex question. A thorough response would fill encyclopedias because it would involve studying innumerable aspects, great and small, of every single human culture around the world. However, for our purposes here, a brief consideration of certain macro-elements of the human experience will suffice.

First let's look at metaphysics: This has already been described as unnatural. Such description may sound negative, but in fact it is not meant to be that, rather merely precise. Metaphysics is concerned not with the natural, but with the supernatural (an element of the unnatural) – and the natural only insofar as it interacts with the supernatural. In judging metaphysics, the first question we should ask is: Does the supernatural exist? If it does, then metaphysics is valid and demonstrably bioferous in that it assists in the expansion of human development into an entirely new plane of existence. However, if the supernatural does not exist, then all models of metaphysics are invalid and misleading, and thus necroferous to some degree depending on the actions of their adherents. Yet even so, considering its enrichment of human thought and other contributions to our well-being and advancement, it would be difficult to argue that metaphysics has not been bioferous in quite a number of ways. That said, we should return to the question of the supernatural's existence.

A thousand years ago, in an era of magic and mystery, the metaphysical realm was a universally accepted fact and had tentacles reaching into all areas of human ignorance, at the time a seemingly all-encompassing domain. By the dawn of the twentieth century this domain had been reduced on many fronts through the efforts of scientists and other thinkers. What remained has since been further reduced and continues daily to be chipped away, bit by bit. Yet this triumphal march of science, while seeming to score victories over metaphysics itself, actually only separates from the supernatural those aspects which never properly should have been attached to it in the first place on account of their being natural phenomena. Thus, paradoxically, science has served to purify metaphysics. Such purification neither validates nor strengthens the metaphysical contention; however, it does assist us in clarifying the matter under investigation – though perhaps not in a very satisfying manner at all. That is to say that the supernatural is, by definition, not natural, and can thus neither be comprehended nor validated, or otherwise judged, by natural means (in other words, by science). This may be annoyingly circular; nevertheless, it is an entirely consistent and defensible position. The result is that we cannot know that the supernatural does not exist, nor can we know that it does exist – unless, of course, it reveals itself to us collectively in an undeniably definite manner. (Revelation, or some such form of enlightenment, is the backbone of all religions; however, to date, all revelations have involved only a chosen few who then pass them on to the masses. Whether or not such revelations are genuine communications from a supernatural realm, they certainly cannot be described as having been revealed – made directly available – to all of mankind collectively in an undeniably definite manner.)

What is the most rational position to take vis-à-vis the question of the supernatural? First of all, whereas the supernatural may exist, the assault on it by science in so many areas, astronomy, biology, medicine, geology and psychiatry, to mention only a few, has so reduced its purview as to relegate it to near-irrelevance. Science's purification of metaphysics is a two-edged sword in that as it weeds out the natural phenomena from the domain of the supernatural, it accordingly reduces the supernatural's practical significance by a commensurate amount.

At any rate, it seems most sensible to avoid according to the supernatural anything natural, and when dealing with the natural to be fastidious in avoiding making reference to the supernatural; yet at the same time, to admit the possibility of the existence of the supernatural, encouraging those among us with the inclination toward pursuing metaphysical thought to make such pursuit. Practically speaking, this means moving from the natural/supernatural hybrid perspective which is prevalent today to a perspective which is wholly natural in focus but allowing for the possibility of a supernatural aspect; such a fundamental realignment will require an enormous amount of introspection, both individual and societal.

We should look at another issue pertaining to metaphysics: purpose. Prior to the conscious awakening of mankind, the issue of purpose was simple: we merely obeyed our instinctive impulses like the rest of biosity, securing and expanding territory, procreating, and preparing our offspring to do the same. Now it is not so simple, and most of this complexity is due to metaphysics. Intertwined with the element of purpose in metaphysical thought we usually find identity and immortality; it is the combination of these three elements which provides the bases for both the guidance mechanisms of individuals and the command structures of societies. Such is the essence of any metaphysical system and the intention here is not to address unanswerable questions like 'Do we have souls?' or 'Is there an afterlife?', particularly considering what an array of perspectives that would involve addressing. Rather, let us identify that common ground regarding purpose shared by all the various metaphysicists, along with non-metaphysicists as well: namely, bioism. A proper understanding of biosity reveals to us the purpose inherent in nature – not an abstract blueprint for past and future envisioned by a supernatural being of higher authority, but instead a built-in drive with the aims of living and expanding the range of biosity, both in time and space. Identifying and accepting the biositic drive as the one common, underlying purpose shared by all of humanity (and shared with all of biosity) does not preclude the possibility of a further, metaphysical purpose for mankind. However, it does provide a sound rational basis for establishing common societal command structures along strictly non-metaphysical lines, leaving individuals the freedom to develop further their own personal (and supplemental) guidance mechanisms based on metaphysical or nonmetaphysical inclinations.

The second major subject we should consider is sensophrenia: As was stated earlier, this encompasses both the pursuit of pleasure and the avoidance of discomfort; and though sensophrenia is a response to biositic urges, the focus of the sensophreniac is so narrow that it cannot be described as bioferous. Considering that Western society is, in many ways, fundamentally sensophrenic, it is impossible to take anything in this subject to its logical conclusion without sounding quite radical in a rather doctrinaire, even puritanical, way. It would take a good long search to find any among us who is not sensophrenic to a degree in some area or other; and it is probably a small minority who do not lead lives oriented primarily toward sensophrenia. Yet while ultimately necroferous in the most immediate sense, it cannot be denied that sensophrenia in the last century or so has been used to good advantage as a motivation tool to lead the masses of humanity onward in numerous great projects, some of which have indubitably been bioferous.

Weighing the merits of sensophrenia, distinguishing clearly the bioferous from the necroferous, is probably the best way to come to a full understanding of bioism, which is nothing other than the underlying philosophy of all biosity – mankind included.

Judging active sensophrenia – pleasure-seeking – is simple: Every pleasure is based on a biositic urge. What differentiates the biocentric satisfaction of a biositic urge from the sensophrenic pursuit of a pleasure is attitude and degree. The biocentric is focused on biosity, whether consciously or otherwise, whereas the sensophreniac has allowed his focus to narrow down to certain elements of biosity rather than the totality. There are two necroferous aspects to the narrowed perspective of the sensophreniac: the first is that even a brief fixation with one biositic urge may lead to an untimely neglect of others, thus endangering the subject; and the second is that any chronic fixation with one urge will lead to an imbalance in the subject which could threaten health or even life. Therefore, on the individual level, active sensophrenia is at best neutral, but generally-speaking necroferous.

We can say much the same about passive sensophrenia as we can of active, merely replacing 'satisfaction of a biositic urge' and 'pursuit of a pleasure' with 'response to a biositic warning' and 'avoidance of a discomfort', although here there are many aspects which at first glance appear not merely neutral but actually bioferous. However, to address passive sensophrenia properly we need to expand our conception of the individual from that of a single entity having roughly a seventy-year lifespan, to that of a single entity with a limited lifespan plus unlimited genetic immortality; this is fundamental to an understanding of bioism. Such an expanded conception casts the avoidance of discomfort in quite a different light, particularly those aspects which would tend to appear bioferous in a seventy year context. Civilizations in general illustrate this nicely. Young civilizations exhibit little concern for pain, fear, fatigue and unpleasant physical sensation; they are aggressive and biocentric. But as civilizations mature, these discomforts are recognized as distractions to their smooth running, and as such are no longer tolerated. The problem with this is that these various aspects of hindrance to a society as a whole are nevertheless stimulants to the strengthening of individuals within that same society; removing them may benefit a civilization in the short-term, but eventually and inescapably the strength of the sum of individuals in a society is reflected in the strength of the society itself. Typically at the time of their decline or collapse civilizations are described as decadent, this usually carrying the connotation of active sensophrenia; but the fact is that while both active and passive sensophrenia are normally present, it is the latter which is the more debilitating because not only is it tolerated and respected, but it is even idealized and made the primary objective as civilizations grow old and disillusioned.

Sensophrenia is not bioferous and can generally be described as necroferous whether we are speaking of individuals or societies. Yet, as noted, it has been instrumental in motivating humanity to progress technologically – in fact, it has likely been far more significant in this regard than bioism itself. Although we could seek a paradox here, perhaps it's more accurate to view such progress rather as evidence of the opportunism of biosity: societies weakened by sensophrenia are overthrown by the more biocentric barbarians who seize the technology oriented toward bioism (that portion which they find comprehensible and sustainable), overlooking or eventually ignoring that of a more sensophrenic nature.

How then shall we deal with sensophrenia so as best to apply the principles of biosity? Ideally, through a thorough understanding of biosity, we would all learn how to motivate ourselves effectively without resort to sensophrenia (since sensophrenia is merely the shadow of biosity). But such a goal may be unrealistic. Perhaps for the foreseeable future a more attainable objective would be to reduce the most necroferous excesses of sensophrenia – those things which directly or indirectly threaten the very wellbeing of humanity and the rest of biosity, whether present or future generations. To do this we must begin by gaining a complete comprehension of sensophrenia, both passive and active, so that we can judge accurately which elements to attack, which to ignore and even which to foster as less necroferous replacements for those that have been useful as motivation tools yet must still be eradicated. Quantifying and qualifying sensophrenia is a massive task in and of itself; but this is nothing compared to taking the resulting conclusions, formulating an implementation strategy and then actually implementing them. Such an endeavor will turn the world as we know it upside-down; yet it should and must be done, for if we do not discipline ourselves and eradicate at least the more necroferous elements of sensophrenia, biosity will do it for us – in its way rather than our own.

The last macro-element of the human experience we should consider in relation to biosity is human progress, referring essentially to civilization, science and technology. This is a very broad topic and the intent here is not to judge between the bioferous and the necroferous, but rather merely to highlight those aspects of human progress which seem most divergent from the norms of biosity and should therefore be the first to be investigated. There are five such aspects, and these are:

1. Implements, from stone tools to interplanetary spacecraft; an example of the sort of question to consider is: Has the advent of the common rifle altered the balance of power between humans and other organisms?

2. Processes, such as agriculture, domestication, urbanization, mining, refining and a host of others.

3. Synthetic substances, which deserve special attention even if we are already considering them when we look at the processes which generate them.

4. Radiation, again something which receives attention in the area of processes, but which nevertheless deserves its own special focus.

5. Medicine, involving a great variety of implements, processes and substances, and being acutely pertinent in the consideration of ethics.

The tone here may give the impression that everything natural is good while everything manmade is bad. This is not the intent. Rather, the intent is to say that everything natural is known to biosity ("known" in the sense that it has been confronted and compensated for – speaking, of course, about those things within the range of biosity), whereas our manmade world is so new that biosity has only just begun to adjust. The point is that manmade things, being unknown to biosity, possess the potential for harm or disruption. Therefore we need to study these things carefully so that the dangers involved can be determined precisely. Then, from a position of knowledge, we can choose the most rational approach in dealing with each aspect. Again, as with sensophrenia, this is an enormous endeavor.

We have now briefly looked at metaphysics, sensophrenia and human progress in general as we consider how to apply the principles of biosity to mankind. Though we have only scratched the surface here, what we have done is very useful for we have seen that in all areas our enemy is ignorance and our first efforts must be directed to the gaining of knowledge. Once we have the necessary knowledge, we can then begin the process of bringing ourselves into conformity with the principles of biosity.

CONCLUSION

Life exists. On this we can all agree. The preceding ideas seek to reduce from life, a physical/metaphysical concept, the purely physical, or scientific, concept of biosity. Assuming this has been accomplished satisfactorily, it becomes apparent that this revised conception of the basis of our existence has far-reaching implications. I have suggested certain actions to be taken, some on the societal level. However, concerning these actions, I have made not the slightest reference to time. This reticence is occasioned by the very ignorance I have pointed out in the final passages. Nevertheless, I want to be clear on my attitude toward the pace of change: I value the incremental approach, seeing it as the most natural; and therefore, the societal changes I suggest here should be undertaken and accomplished not in the context of years, but rather in the context of decades and perhaps even centuries.

BIOTHEISM

Life in the beginning was a point in the nullity, the only point in the nullity of time and space. There was nothing, either physical or metaphysical, in the beginning apart from this point in the nullity that was life. This point in the nullity was everything: all being, all force, all understanding. Life, this point in the nullity, was and is God.

Out of this beginning, this point in the nullity, arose the universe in its totality. By fiat, life summoned matter into being. At this moment of fiat God was dynamically omniscient and omnipotent. Since then God's omniscience and omnipotence have been latent. God's omnipresence has been unchanged from the beginning.

*　　　*　　　*

Long ago there was a village with a very deep well. In fact, this well was so deep that its bottom had never been reached. This led someone to suggest that the well was bottomless, but at first nobody took such an idea seriously. As the years and centuries advanced and human knowledge and curiosity progressed, this village and its well came to be known far and wide among men of learning. A competition grew up as to who could plumb its depth and locate its bottom. With increasing ingenuity, magicians, philosophers, wise men, alchemists, thinkers and at last, in modern times, scientists attacked the mystery. The measurements became enormous and vast amounts of knowledge were gained about many things, but to this day nobody has found the well's bottom. Many people now believe this well to be bottomless, and of course many others believe quite the opposite; but perhaps most surprisingly, the vast majority of people are so taken with the process, that is to say the measurements and the peripheral knowledge, that they have forgotten or all but forgotten the still unanswered question that got it all started.

This village well story leads me to a couple questions which I will propose and then answer toward demonstrating a rational philosophical basis for metaphysical belief. Having read 'Biosity', you are probably thinking that its author would be the last person to make such an argument. It is true that I consider most religiosity to be little more than superstition, most religion to be functionally little more than crowd control, and most religious contentions to have been overthrown by science. It is not without reason that atheists say with increasing confidence that God is dead. However, although metaphysics may be, and is by definition, a matter of faith, paradoxically, the rejection or absence of metaphysical belief is equally based and dependent on faith. So faith then is a matter not of unthinking passivity, but rather of the careful sifting of observable reality and the choosing of that model of reality which most rationally addresses the indiscernible. Metaphysics is unavoidable.

Here is my first question: What is the source of all matter, of the material realm? Theists would readily respond by naming God as the source, whereas atheists would deny that there is a source. In contrast to both of these positions, agnostics would merely say that this cannot be known.

There are three types of theists: monotheists, polytheists and pantheists. Polytheism is untenable, and so it is nothing more than creeping monotheism. Monotheists conceptualize God in metaphysical terms as being apart from the material realm. Pantheists conceptualize the material realm in totality as being synonymous with God; therefore to pantheists the material realm is God eternal without origin. Interestingly, this leaves pantheists with a position here functionally similar to that of atheists in that for both the material realm is eternal without origin.

Like pantheists, agnostics too have a position here that is functionally similar to that of atheists because, in ostensibly not taking a position they necessarily adopt the conservative default position which says that it was as it is. Thus practically-speaking for agnostics the material realm is eternal without origin.

Let's move on to my second question: Who or what is the inherent authority in the universe? Theists would readily respond by naming God, whereas atheists would deny that there is any inherent authority. Agnostics again would merely say that this cannot be known.

The position of monotheists is straightforward: God is the inherent authority in the universe. At first glance, that of pantheists is similarly clear. However, pantheists, upon further reflection, would be forced to concede that because everything is God, therefore equally authoritative, nothing is inherently any more authoritative than anything else; so that there is functionally no authority. This leaves pantheists again with a position similar practically to that of atheists who outright deny that there is any inherent authority.

Like pantheists, agnostics again have a position here that is functionally similar to that of atheists. As with the previous question, in ostensibly not taking a position here they necessarily adopt the conservative default position – in this case the position which says that no authority may be acknowledged. Functionally this is equivalent to there being no inherent authority.

First cause and authority are the only two integral issues when considering God. One's positions on these two issues define one's ultimate stance on the question of God. Although at first glance it would appear that the field is divided into three camps, atheists, theists and agnostics, in fact it is divided into only two: theists and atheists. Theists include monotheists and polytheists who, as has been noted, are creeping monotheists. Atheists include atheists proper, pantheists (who are creeping atheists) and agnostics (who are also creeping atheists). Just as polytheism is an untenable stance, so too are pantheism and agnosticism.

We are left with two tenable stances on the question of God: atheism and monotheism. Let us consider them: If one believes that there is no God then one by default must accept the belief in material eternality and all that entails to maintain a rational position. Material eternality means that no matter has ever been created or come into being; all of it has always existed, merely fluctuating in form, describable but ultimately not explainable (as a whole); and the thirteen billion or so years since the Big Bang – not to mention the six decades or so since Hiroshima – is a mere blip in the span of eternity. Moreover, this incredibly intricate and complex structure of reality around us and of which we are part, which the accumulated human thought of centuries has found to be in obedience to a body of laws rationally described, was not constituted by any rational being or force, but rather merely is, exists. On the other hand, with God you have an extrapolation unobservable by scientific means: this is its only problem, yet philosophically-speaking this is not a problem since such an extrapolation is by definition outside of the material realm and its tools of observation. This is not to say that this gives the metaphysical model a greater likelihood of being correct than the materialistic. Both rest on sound reasoning and each has its own incomprehensibility. Interestingly, the one cannot be proved without disproving the other, and the other by its internal structure cannot be disproved. Thus, either way, we are left with a matter of faith, rationally-defensible faith.

However, there is more to consider here than simply internal logic. Both monotheism and atheism have grave inadequacies. No monotheist to date has ever come up with a reasonable description of God's purpose. For what reason would an omnipotent and omniscient Being create the universe? Is there some need or desire that God had? And could the interaction that an omniscient and omnipotent God has supposedly had with us sentient beings be anything other than a game? How could it be otherwise in light of divine sovereignty? Is there any tenable way to square divine sovereignty and human free will? These are just some of the questions that monotheists hide from behind the cover of the incomprehensibility of God. There are no answers here, just inadequacy. The monotheists have no answers.

What about the atheists? They certainly relish making the same points about monotheism made here, all of these and more. But what about the inadequacies of their stance? Allusion has already been made to this complex structure of reality of which we are part, which according to atheists was not constituted by any rational being or force. This is very problematic. Even more problematic is their disregard of will. Atheists have every bit as much difficulty with will and being as monotheists have with divine sovereignty and human free will. There is no place in their simplistic reduction of reality to material terms for the existence of will. Yet will exists. Being exists. Beings exist. Atheists have no answers here, only a fundamental inadequacy.

Pantheism as discussed above is not life-centered. Rather, it is inclusive of all matter whether organic or not. This is abiocentric pantheism. In contrast to this I would like to introduce biotheism. Biotheism is biocentric pantheism, the belief that life is God. Biotheism is not only a form of pantheism, but in fact the only form of pantheism that is viable. Life per se is God, but the rest of reality is an outgrowth of God, thus the pantheistic element.

Unlike abiocentric pantheism, biotheism is not creeping atheism. Biotheism identifies a source of all matter: God. Biotheism not only identifies such source, but even locates the time and place that matter came into being: the Big Bang. There is no functional similarity between biotheism's identification of God as the source of all matter and atheism's eternal material realm without origin.

As to the question of the inherent authority in the universe, again biotheism stands in stark contrast to atheism. Although to the biotheist everything is an outgrowth of God, it is life per se that is God, that is the inherent authority in the universe. To atheists there is no inherent authority. To the biotheist there is, both theoretically and functionally. Whereas abiocentric pantheism is creeping atheism, biotheism – biocentric pantheism – is not.

Biotheism is viable as a form of theism. As such it does not have to address the inadequacies of atheism. However, it does have to address the inadequacies of theism.

Does biotheism square divine sovereignty and human free will? Yes. God's omniscience and omnipotence, having been embedded in the fabric of the universe, are latent. It is now only through the exertion of will by living beings that such omniscience and omnipotence are expressed; and such expression is constrained by the limitations of the channels in which it moves. Moreover, unlike in the regular conception of theists, in the conception of the biotheist God does not know the future, God's omniscience does not extend to future events. In biotheism omniscience extends only to what exists. The future does not exist, and therefore cannot be known. This overcomes a cheat normally found in theism that turns the whole interaction of God and creation into a mere game. These two concepts together, God's latent omniscience and omnipotence and the non-existence of the future, enable biotheism to reconcile divine sovereignty and human free will.

What is the purpose of the universe? Purpose per se is necessarily a metaphysical concept. Since it is a formulation of will, and will is part and parcel of being, purpose cannot exist, come into existence, independent of being. There can be no purpose where there is no purposer – in this universal sense, Purposer. So purpose, like authority, is a concept available only to the theist and denied to the atheist. Biotheism offers no complete answer to this question of purpose. By looking at life we can vaguely see the exertion of will, its spread in both space and time. Clearly there is an underlying purpose driving this process. Could this be evidence of some sort of divine self-actualization exercise? This seems like a good starting point for understanding here. However, any answer beyond this is speculative. Suffice to say that, unlike other theists, most or all of whom base their understanding of purpose on one or another of various sources of purportedly divine revelation, the biotheist depends on reason alone, interpreting the underlying patterns of reality he sees as manifestations of God's purpose, thus basing his formulations of divine purpose entirely on his perceptions of reality.

Within the tenable stance on the question of God that is theism, the biotheistic alternative overcomes the inadequacies inherent in the monotheistic perspective. Unlike all other approaches to the metaphysical – atheism included, biotheism is not only viable and tenable, but it is adequate as well.

Biotheism reconciles the physical and the metaphysical, demonstrating that the physical is the metaphysical. God is dead. Long live God! ¡Viva la Vida!

BIOFEROSITY:

THE NEW STANDARD OF MORALITY

Reason through science has overthrown the old standards of morality or relegated them to the realm of metaphysics. We are left today with the shifting sands of relativity. We have no foundation for the ordering of society, and an underlying sense of moral confusion reigns. Yesterday's virtue is today's shame; and today's vice will be tomorrow's cause. Such rudderlessness is undesirable, even potentially disastrous. We, society, humanity, need a common measuring stick of right and wrong. To continue otherwise is to invite, or tolerate, fragmentation and conflict.

Unless or until such time as all of mankind adheres to a single code of metaphysical belief, no such model of morality is valid as the common basis for human interaction. We must adopt a standard of morality based on observation and reason rather than religious faith. "Bioferosity" is just such a standard. No longer do we need to describe "good" in the light of godliness, happiness or pleasure – or some juggling of these and other ill-defined qualities. Now we have bioferosity: that which is bioferous is good or right; whereas that which is necroferous is bad or wrong. There will still be vigorous debate as to the interpretation of data, but no more will we have the kaleidoscopic wildcard of metaphysics overshadowing the issues, obscuring our vision and sapping our energy.

Basing morality on bioferosity doesn't result in any sort of cut-and-dried rulebook of right and wrong. For instance, looking at wolves and sheep, how would one judge when to support the interests of one group as opposed to those of the other? However, what can be surely stated is that life is made up of entities, and it is the nature of an entity that its own self interest is paramount – otherwise it would not be an entity, rather, only part of an entity. Using this understanding as a basis to proceed from, we can develop sets of priorities that begin to show a rational framework for morality. The following three priority lists reflect three different focuses: individuals, societies and humanity as a whole. The one for individuals is the most natural, and thus perhaps reflects the deepest reality. The other two, purely-speaking, engender conflicts of interest when added to the first, but in practice these conflicts involve additional benefits which ultimately reinforce the priorities in the primary list.

Priority List One – Individual Perspective:

1. The survival of life in general
2. The survival of the human race

3. The survival of one's society

4. The survival of oneself

5. The survival of one's offspring (because they are one's genetic posthumous survival)

6. The survival of one's parents (because being positioned as their genetic posthumous survival, one is naturally placed higher in their interests than in anyone else's)

7. The survival of one's siblings (because shared genetics positions them as alternate routes of one's genetic posthumous survival)

8. The survival of one's friends, related or otherwise (because one's own survival is presumably somewhat in their immediate interests)

9. The survival of individual members of one's society (because communal interests necessitate that one's survival is generally to some degree in their interests)

10. The survival of individuals outside one's own society (because one's survival may be to some slight degree in their interests)

11. The survival of individual organisms outside the human race

This is a preliminary list. In fact, the well-being – as opposed to mere survival – of oneself and one's friends and family likely would come higher than the last two or three listed priorities, and the survival of entire species (besides humanity) would certainly be somewhere higher than the last stated priority.

Priority List Two – Society Perspective:

1. The survival of life in general
2. The survival of the human race
3. The survival of the society
4. The survival of individual members of the society
5. The survival of individuals outside the society
6. The survival of individual organisms outside the human race

Priority List Three – Humanity Perspective:

1. The survival of life in general
2. The survival of the human race
3. The survival of individual members of the human race
4. The survival of individual organisms outside the human race

Careful research and analysis should yield refined priority lists, or even one integrated list, that need never be changed, lists that so accurately reflect the reality – in contrast to the ideal – of the knowable subject biosity that they carry almost the same weight as the laws of science. Such a list or lists will comprise the first building blocks of the new and sustainable morality based on bioferosity.

Our new standard of morality will directly affect many aspects of our lives. Medical ethics will receive some desperately needed direction. The legal system will become the child of reason rather than the creature of machination that it is today. Some degree of universally-accepted etiquette can be reintroduced into our day-to-day relations with one another. Lifelong forms of self-discipline, in areas such as food consumption, substance use, exercise, employment and material consumerism, among others, will be devised and adopted with confidence. And government will be restructured to become fully and permanently aligned with biosity. All of these, and many other things, will be effected by the adoption of bioferosity as our standard of morality.

The old ways are gone. Humanism has left us rudderless, tossed by every wind. Bioferosity offers us a new way, the rational way that we need. We must seize it, being prepared to embark on its lengthy and ever-ongoing implementation.

GARY WILSON

CONTROL

Like so many people, I used to hate and fear communism, that monstrous system of totalitarianism. I saw it as the very incarnation of evil. What a relief then it was when a decade ago it ran out of steam and collapsed.

No longer feeling menaced by communism, I can now look at it with objectivity, far moreso than I could back then. No more do I see it as inherently evil, but rather as inherently flawed. I can now appreciate the sincere idealism that was its driving force, and distinguish between the revolutionaries who swept away a corrupt ruling class and the pragmatists who became the new ruling class (and swept away the revolutionaries in the process). Most of all, I have come to the understanding that communism was above all else a system of control – and in realizing this it dawned on me that every other system, every other society, is first and foremost a system of control. The underlying things we hold in unquestioning awe, equality, human rights, the contract, democracy, the rule of law, carry no divine sanction or historical inevitability: rather, they are merely tools, tools in our own and other systems of control.

The difference between traditional and modern societies is that traditional societies evolved over time as the result of competing interests, whereas their modern counterparts developed as the products of conscious design based on widely-accepted principles. In light of this distinction, one could say that the first prototypical modern societies were theocracies established by priesthoods – in which case it is interesting to speculate on whether the priests themselves took their divine pronouncements seriously or cynically recognized them for what they were: control mechanisms. The age of enlightenment has led us into the mainstream of modernity. This is when the great principles fundamental to all of Western society were formulated most extensively, and oriented toward reason rather than divine revelation. Yet even these great principles, try as we might to dress them up in the trappings of secularism, have been at heart dependent on metaphysical premises. Look at equality: Here is a concept that no serious politician or statesman would dare to question. What is it based on? The doctrine that all are equal in the sight of God. Does it perhaps have a parallel basis that is purely secular? No, without reference to a higher authority the concept of equality is a dogma, its own authority. How can we say that all are equal when if any one of us were forced to choose between saving the life of a loved one or that of a complete stranger we would choose to save the loved one, thus demonstrating the inequality of the value we place on the two lives? Or how about if we make society the higher authority?

Should any society value all its members equally, placing on a par the unskilled laborer who can easily be replaced by any of ten million others with the astrophysicist, or pre-eminent heart surgeon, or military genius, who cannot be replaced by anyone, or poorly at best by maybe a dozen lesser peers? To that question the pat answer is yes, but the honest answer is no – and in fact this is demonstrated quite clearly by the difference in the levels of health care afforded to leading politicians and regular citizens. About the only other potential secular basis for equality is biology, the fact that all we humans are of the same species sharing a common physical and mental make-up; however, the plain fact is that similarity and equality are two separate things and the presence of the one doesn't necessarily signify the presence of the other. To accept equality then as an unquestionable good, we must resort to metaphysics; and if, as I maintain, one's metaphysical beliefs should not be used in the controlling of others, meaning that in establishing the structures of society no reference whatsoever should be made to metaphysics, then even this basis is for all means and purposes invalid and we are left with a dogma.

The great principles of Western society, the sacred tenets of humanism, are all, like equality, dogmas. We want to accept them as the products of reason, but in reality they are the children of metaphysics and only adopted by reason. This is not to condemn these concepts in and of themselves. The fact is that they have been undeniably beneficial. Rather, it is to call for a reformulated perception of them: No longer should we view them dogmatically as self-evident truths, authorities unto themselves. Instead we must take them for exactly what they are, tools, and employ them accordingly.

Liberty and security are the two principal urges of humanity. We all want to be able to do whatever we want. We all want to be safe. These two desires sometimes complement each other, and at other times are in direct opposition to each other. More than anything else, it is the conflict between them that has led to the rise of highly-organized societies. An individual utterly detached from all society is in one sense perfectly at liberty, yet he is so weakened by such detachment – he must count only upon himself for his own defence, he has no safety net in time of injury or sickness and his possessions are limited to those things which he can immediately defend – that he has less actual liberty than most socialized individuals who have surrendered great swaths of liberty in return for the security to enjoy more completely other, retained liberties.

The foundation of any society is the social contract. Historically, most such contracts have been unwritten and entirely lacking in any systematic exposition of their elements; the parties to them gained comprehension of their elements much in the same way as one learns a language. Even the more recent, written social contracts seldom clearly express all their elements and are still learned more through experience than formal education. As with any other contract, the elements of a social contract can be divided into two groups: rights and responsibilities. Also as with any other contract, if a person is in a state of acceptance of a particular social contract – no matter how grudgingly – it is fair and proper to say that the rights of that contract are in balance with the responsibilities, even if this does not appear to an onlooker to be the case. Being the embodiment of a set of rights and responsibilities, the social contract is a tool of control: it controls you and your fellow members of society, telling you the scope of what you can do, your liberty, and the scope of the conduct you can expect from others, your security. It is the fundamental control tool on which all others are based.

Perhaps the most important control tool after the social contract is property. The concept of property is so ingrained in Western society that most people take it entirely for granted, accepting it as a divinely-sanctioned right or describing it as an expression of natural law. Nevertheless, it is just a tool, nothing more, nothing less. Possession is a fact; property, being societally-authorized possession, is a tool. And it is an immensely useful tool because, being employed for the designation of control in a sphere, it can be applied to any and every sphere of control under the sway of a society. Land and material property, being the most ancient and tangible forms of property, are often taken far more seriously than various other forms, yet this is so mainly because one's possession of these things can normally be demonstrated and defended with little or no recourse to the more sophisticated structures of a society's system of enforcement. Less tangible forms of property, such as radio frequencies, patents and powers of monopoly, are every bit as valid, and often of far more value. Contracts, also representing the designation of control – usually covering the exchange of a right, good or service for money or a different right, good or service, are another form of property, and a particularly interesting form in that they are so versatile and modifiable.

Let me now return to where we started: the evaluation of communism and systems of control in general. Throughout the latter half of the twentieth century we had a leftwing/rightwing paradigm that tried to fit every society under consideration somewhere on its spectrum. I think most people knew at the time that this model of reality wasn't natural or sustainable long-term, but for that era, having a bipolar world with communism on one side and capitalism on the other, it was useful. However, that was then and this is now – and we definitely need a new model, one that is based on reason and thus permanently sustainable, rather than one that arises or is devised solely for some immediate purpose.

Control is important. It is vital. While it may be tempting to denounce all government as bad and say that everyone should be free to do what he wants without interference, this is quite unrealistic. Anarchy is much closer akin to chaos and death than to liberty and life. Every society is based on control and has various tools of control. What we must do is orient ourselves so that we are able to recognize and fully comprehend all these tools of control and then employ them in the best possible way. And how do we determine what is the best possible way? Here we refer back to bioferosity. This must be our underlying standard of good and bad, right and wrong, in ordering society: the way of life, that which ultimately brings life to a society, is the ultimate good, whereas the way of death, that which ultimately brings death to a society, is the ultimate bad.

There are many necroferous things in Western society, both in our control structures and elsewhere. Yet our civilization is the strongest and arguably the most bioferous ever; and this is due to the previously-described metaphysical-cum-rational dogmas on which it is based more than anything else. Why is this so? Why are these dogmas which we have lowered from their pedestals and relegated to the status of tools the basis of the strongest, most bioferous societies in human history? Because it just so happens that the sum total effect of these dogmas is to create the conditions most favorable to the higher development of the greatest attribute of humanity: reason. The one thing that distinguishes humans from other animals is the power of the human mind; yet when we live in a hand-to-mouth existence or are in that state of constant subliminal terror used by many societies as a means of control, our ability to develop reason and our minds is horrendously inhibited. The great dogmas of Western society encourage the greatest number of people to develop their minds to the greatest extent, and this is why our society is so strong. Equality and democracy do two things: they create a bond of trust between each member of society and the society itself as a whole, giving the members confidence not only in the benevolence of the society but also in the value of their own expenditures of effort; and they provide a context in which well-developed minds can gain rewards and influence. Property and contracts, by clearly designating control throughout various spheres and activities, do three things: they reduce conflicts; they foster predictability, thus encouraging the confidence of members of a society in the future and the attendant value of expending effort toward long-term goals; and they guarantee the benefits of a thing to those responsible for it. Finally we have the rule of law, and again, like the other dogmas, its value as a tool to society relates to the bond of trust it creates between the society and its members, and the predictability and confidence it inspires in its members so that the hand-to-mouth mindset can be left behind and monumental endeavors, whether group or individual, can be undertaken. In all these things the consistent thread is confidence. The development of the human body, along with primal mental activity similar to that of animals, occurs naturally and proceeds without conscious effort. The development of the human mind is another matter entirely: it does not occur naturally; it requires a constant conscious effort; and it takes a tremendous amount of time. Any society wherein there is no sure confidence that the time and effort devoted to mental development and achievement will pay off can expect to see a minimum of such development and achievement.

In every society control is inevitable. Rather than fearing and seeking to eliminate the tools of control, we must understand and employ them in the very best way we can. Perhaps some will in fact be eliminated. Perhaps others than what we currently have will be developed. Whatever we do, we must orient ourselves according to the standard of bioferosity so that our decisions are guided by what most encourages life, and this for both the near future all but upon us and the more distant degrees of future, each concealed progressively moreso from our sight.

GARY WILSON

DEMOCRACY:

WILL IS THE ESSENCE OF LIFE

Democracy has come so completely into vogue over the last centuries that few today would dare to criticize it or promote any other form of government. The belief in the value or goodness of democracy, its unquestioned superiority over the alternatives, has become a modern dogma. Those living in democracies take for granted the rightness and inevitability of its spread worldwide. Whereas those living in non-democratic countries, depending on what they have to gain or lose, either give lip service to it and its trappings so as to guard against and forestall its actual coming, or hope for the genuine realization of it.

It is fair to say that democracy has become a dogma in and of itself. For all practical purposes, this is an accurate statement. However, we can also look deeper and see that democracy is in turn based on equality. Now, equality truly is a dogma, properly-speaking. It is an irreducible concept that must be taken on faith, or similarly rejected. What makes it particularly compelling and powerful is that it can be found quite clearly in both secular and metaphysical systems of thought. Since it thus can be furthered by adherents of differing philosophies working together, and is often doubly reinforced within those who have syncretistic tendencies, its spread as a concept has been wide and profoundly influential. None of this changes the fact that it is still at heart a dogma, a premise that must be, and is, taken on faith. Within metaphysical systems the basis of authority for this premise is a supernatural being or force, clearly a faith issue. Conversely, within secular systems the basis is similarity, the relative uniformity of the members of our species, and at first glance this is not a faith issue, but rather purely a matter of reason. What makes it a faith issue are the imperatives that are then implied. It is one thing to say that a human being from such-and-such a place is the biological equivalent of another from somewhere halfway around the globe – this is purely rational and requires no faith, only observation and comparison; it is quite another to develop from there that these two individuals should be treated equivalently, in the general sense and particularly the political.

These imperatives are the theory based on the facts, and as such are fundamentally a matter of faith; moreover, in this particular instance there is a further, specific faith issue in that biological equivalency alone is accepted as the degree of similarity necessary as the standard of uniformity.

Having noted all this, let it be clearly understood that the intent here is not the undermining or overthrow of the concept and ideals of democracy, but instead its reformulation on a rational, rather than dogmatic, basis. Why is it that the comprehensive growth of democracy observable today has come about only in the present era? Are the current and most recent generations so morally superior to their forefathers as to explain this? Has history been carrying us inexorably toward this – or some more complete – apex of political maturity? Or is the prevailing manifestation of widespread democracy just a happy accident in our time, a conjunction of benign influences, fragile as glass and fated to come to an end like all other good things? The answer to this line of questioning is quite simply that modern democracy, like so many other things, is the product of the machine age. Why? Because the advent of machines has emphasized and enhanced that aspect of the human species which is our unique and overwhelming strength: the mind. Whereas machines perform tasks which would for the most part require great human skill and/or effort, these same machines yet need to be controlled by us humans. It is this control of machines that has been the great leveller. A person today can spend a relatively short period of time learning and perfecting the control of a machine so as to produce with it things of value that a medieval craftsman could not have produced in his entire life, or work output that no medieval could have matched in twenty times the hours laboring. Machine control elevates the value, the marketable value, of the human mind and diminishes the value of physical strength, even highly-skilled physical strength. Thus, it is simple economics that has dictated the flourishing of equality, therefore, democracy. The masses have drawn nearer to the various surviving specialized elites, close enough that political delineation is no longer feasible. This is no fragile development teetering on the brink of oblivion. Democracy is the form of government which best appreciates and harnesses the totality of minds it represents; as such, it embodies the combined power of its members' greatest strength: their reason.

This brings us back to the previously-considered standard of uniformity: biological equivalency. When we look at this in the context of controlling machines, it becomes apparent that biological equivalency, with particular reference to the mind, is sufficiently narrow in scope that it is indeed a feasible standard of uniformity, for the time being, on which we can base theory. The average person, with a reasonable amount of training, can control the average machine. (This is not to elevate machine control to some hallowed status of significance – it is just a handy yardstick for revealing and highlighting the functional uniformity of the human mind across the entire species.) Here then we have a sound basis on which we can begin to build, guided less by ideals to be taken on faith and more by objectives to be pursued in light of experience.

Let us shift gears now and relate this to bioism. Considering that our underlying aim is the furtherance of life in general, and that of our species and ourselves in particular, we must orient our objectives accordingly. What is the essence of life? What is it that distinguishes animate from inanimate matter? Volition. Will is the essence of life. It follows, then, that the system of government which most embodies the will of its citizens, and which most employs and encourages the development of that will, is the system most aligned with biosity – with life itself. Democracy, the mass expression of volition, is just such a system.

When we use the word "democracy," what do we mean? In the ancient Greek democracies the vast majority of the population had no vote or say in government; likewise in late medieval England (in the centuries immediately after Magna Carta). In America's early years various requirements barred many from participating; and we were well into the twentieth century before women could vote throughout most of the democratic world. Should we then exclude all these embryonic or developing forms of democracy when we consider or discuss democracy proper? No, because at the heart of all of them was the focus on the will of the people, imperfectly as it may have been enfranchised or expressed.

Advancing the will of the people is the heart of democracy, though not necessarily its direct strength. The strength of democracy is three-fold and a by-product of the process of advancing the people's will:

- by incorporating flexibility of leadership, democracy offers those persons most suited to lead the possibility of the opportunity to lead – it accesses a vast pool of potential talent that is inherently denied to other systems;

- by providing all citizens a say in government, even if only small, democracy thereby legitimately establishes responsibility and loyalty to the state; and

- in demonstrating respect toward the will of the individual (albeit collectively), democracy allows and encourages the exercise and further development of will on the individual level.

The first two of these directly strengthen a democracy's government, while the third enriches and empowers the individuals within a democracy, which in turn further strengthens the democracy itself.

At this point it is clear that it should be our purpose both to protect democracy and to further develop and perfect it. It may sound incongruous to emphasize democracy's inherent strength and then to talk about protecting it, yet there are various threats that must be guarded against. Even the most robust man can be felled by things so diverse and lacking in forewarning as an invisible virus or a stray arrow. What are some of the threats to democracy? External enemies of the human variety, whether on the individual and small-group level (i.e. terrorism) or as represented by foreign states. Internal enemies of the human variety, as exemplified by crime and lawlessness; and by corruption, particularly dangerous in that its practitioners are generally cloaked in all respectability and responsibility. Much less obviously, by the sort of monopoly which, if left unregulated, contains the potential to control the democratic will or mechanisms. Any threat to humanity is a threat in turn to democracy: Environmental upheaval, whether the result of human activity (pollution, species extinction et cetera) or natural phenomena (climate shift, solar activity, meteorites et cetera). Epidemic or pandemic disease. Unbridled technological development (synthesized carcinogens, nuclear weapons, superhuman intelligence et cetera). A democracy must acknowledge and combat, to whatever extent is reasonable, all of these threats and others or it is entrusting its future to chance.

The one mentioned threat that deserves specific further attention is superhuman intelligence. By this is meant artificial intelligence. Sometime in the first couple decades of the twenty-first century, computers will surpass the human mind (in overall ability). This is a Rubicon that should be understood before it is crossed. Will this subvert democracy by eroding the feasibility of using the mind and its control of machines as the standard of biological equivalency? Will this allow the few to rule the many by replacing democracy with technocracy? Will this ultimately allow life to develop into an inorganic form, leaving humanity by the wayside in the process? Which is the higher aim: democracy or technology? In the furtherance of life, what is the best path to follow? Whereas it is clear that one should have misgivings as to the goodness of too highly developed artificial intelligence, no answers here are being suggested to the preceding questions. The point is that much investigation and analysis must be done in this area and should be done before the decisions are out of our hands.

As for further developing and perfecting democracy, the essential goal is to maximize the ability of all citizens to exercise their will. On the one hand this means maximizing their liberty, and on the other it means maximizing their input – and ability to input – into the decision-making process on the governmental level.

An argument for greater liberty is not ipso facto an argument against governmental control. When the government disallows robbery, it may be placing a check on the activities of highwaymen, but at the same time it is providing far greater liberty for the vast majority of citizens. Medicare and the welfare state may involve a tax burden, thus an infringement on economic liberty, but by reducing the uncertainty and fear of economic disaster stemming from health and certain other problems, liberty overall is greatly enhanced. This whole area represents the primary focus of political debate today, the basis of the political spectrum, and no attempt will be made here to delineate an optimum position. Sincerity and good faith are found from one end of this spectrum to the other. Enough to say that the objective is to heighten the ability to exercise will at the individual level.

With the spread of democracy around the globe and the increased franchise in long-existing democracies, it is fair to say that great progress has been made in the last century toward maximizing the input of the masses, both real and potential, into the governmental decision-making process. However, this is not something that can ever be finished, perfected, once and for all. Rather, it is an ongoing process that continually evolves along with society. The biggest factor driving this evolution is technology. The growing interactivity and network of society carries opportunities in many ways of increasing the input of the people into government. It is not only desirable, but even incumbent upon us, to seize these opportunities; otherwise, we risk the danger of allowing democracy to succumb to calcification and eventual fossilization.

One final point should be made as to the global scope of democracy. Considering that the biological equivalency of mankind, with particular reference to the mind as the standard of uniformity, is the basis of equality and therefore democracy, it becomes clear that a system of democracy – any and every one – must ultimately be open to include all members of the human race. While it is valid for a system to place restrictions, including outright exclusion, on persons lacking loyalty to it or lacking the maturity necessary to participate in it, such restrictions must be seen as nothing more than unavoidable and temporary steps in the evolution toward the perfect equality of all mankind and must be applied sincerely and with reluctance. Neither geography nor the accident of birth should allow us to delude ourselves on this point.

OUTLINE OF GOVERNMENT

The most perfect government most perfectly embodies the will of the people. Every aspect of the state, every aspect of government, is built upon, stems from, the people, the root of the state.

A tree is an excellent metaphor for government. From the root rises the trunk, and out from the trunk spread the branches. In the following model, the trunk of government, the votive trunk, is the elected body whose task it is to represent and uphold the will of the people with a diversity of voices in a manner that has an overall unity. Distinct from, yet dependent on, the votive trunk are the different branches of government: the legislative branch, the judicial branch and the various executive branches.

THE VOTIVE TRUNK

The votive trunk is composed of a single elected body, the parliament. This body has three hundred members, each serving a three-year term. Elections of these members are staggered and held annually, so that each year one hundred members are elected. Elections are conducted on a proportional basis to insure that every citizen has an equal vote regardless of geography or other considerations. All citizens vote each year, and elections are held on the same date each year.

The tasks of the votive trunk are to authorize all government taxation and spending; to appoint all decision-makers within the branches of government; and to maintain the ongoing fitness of the constitution.

The underlying principle to be followed in the area of taxation is that taxation absent cause is illegitimate. Government may be overwhelmingly the largest service-provider in society, yet it is a service-provider all the same and its citizens are no less entitled to business-like treatment from it than they are from any other service-provider they use. Every single instance of taxation must be linked directly to the service or body of services it finances. When parliament authorizes spending in some branch or division of government, it must also authorize the taxation necessary to cover that spending and assign such taxation specifically to the beneficiaries of the service funded by the spending. In some cases these beneficiaries are all of the citizens, in others they are all corporations, in others just a few citizens or corporations et cetera. Whatever the case may be, the taxation must be sufficient, it must be transparent and it must be specifically warranted.

The votive trunk appoints all decision-makers throughout government. This is an enormous power. Every judge, from the lowest courts all the way up to the supreme court, is appointed by parliament. Similarly, every legislator of the thousand-member legislature and every head of every executive branch, along with the division heads within the branches, is so appointed. Though great, this power of appointment is not absolute. Each session of parliament appoints only a hundred of the thousand legislators and only one of the supreme court judges. Lesser judges are appointed for life and can be removed only with an extraordinary two-thirds majority vote of impeachment.

The constitution is the fundamental written document of the state. It outlines the purpose and role of government, and defines the rights and responsibilities of the citizens. The stability of the constitution is critical to the stability of the state; yet stability must be balanced against adaptability, for when times change it is equally critical that the state be able to adapt as needed. The composition of the constitution is entirely the province of the votive trunk. It is as illegitimate for the legislature to write laws not in conformity with, or outside the parameters set by, the constitution as it is for the judiciary likewise to interpret them. The regular method of constitutional amendment is for four consecutive annual sessions of parliament to vote their approval with a simple majority; this ensures stability while still providing for adaptability. However, constitutional amendment is also possible via an extraordinary three-quarters majority vote of parliament, ensuring that the state cannot be caught flatfooted in time of dire urgency.

In any event, it is valid for certain elements of the constitution to be made more fixed and thus to require higher vote majorities than the above described.

THE LEGISLATIVE BRANCH

The legislative branch is composed of a single appointed body, the legislature. This body has one thousand members. There is no pre-determined length of term for any member; however, members should enter the legislature ready to serve there for life. Legislators are appointed by parliament. Each year, at the end of its annual session, parliament appoints one hundred legislators. These replace those legislators who have died, retired or resigned in the last year, as well as a further number of legislators parliament simultaneously chooses for dismissal. (In the event more than one hundred legislators have left, parliament appoints an appropriate number to bring the legislature to one thousand members and makes no simultaneous dismissals.) In this way the legislature is a stable, long term reflection of the votive trunk, yet incompetent, misguided or unproductive legislators are weeded out without disruption. Anyone who has served as a judge, parliamentarian or tenured professor of law may be appointed to the legislature.

The primary task of the legislature is to write all the laws within the state, and to do so in conformity with the constitution. Toward this end the legislature must be a storehouse of information, knowledge, understanding and wisdom. While the specialization of legislators and the use of committees are valid, all laws must receive the majority approval of the legislature as a whole to come into effect. For the legislature to be effective, legislators must monitor closely three things: the spheres of control and related activities their laws affect; the court rulings based on those laws; and any amendments to the constitution which necessitate amendments to those laws. All law must be written by legislators unaided by staff, special interest groups or lobbyists; however, it is reasonable that legislative staff aid in research. The legislature must always keep in mind that the purpose of the law is to guide the citizenry in conducting itself in a right manner – that is to say, in accordance with the constitution; and to guide the judiciary in settling disputes arising out of the conduct of the citizenry. This means that the law must be both clear and intelligible to citizenry and judiciary alike.

The one other task of the legislature is to nominate three of its own members each year for consideration by parliament in its appointment of a supreme court judge.

THE EXECUTIVE BRANCHES

There are six executive branches: the human rights authority; the economic rights authority; the mass communication authority; the spatial rights authority; the property rights authority; and the societal rights authority. These six correspond to the six categories of spheres of control found within the state. Each of these branches is composed of a number of divisions, each division representing a distinct sphere of control or function within a sphere.

The human rights authority deals with those spheres of control which relate to each citizen's person as an individual. It has three divisions: the person division, the political division and the family division. The person division covers perhaps the most primal of all spheres of control: the integrity of the person, one's right to total control over one's own physical body and mind. Included as necessary elements within this sphere of control are personal space, more or less of which depending on the circumstances, and more specifically, the domicile and perhaps the private vehicle as extensions of one's inviolable space. (Regarding the domicile, a maximum allowable size must be set

– in the range of one acre total of interior and exterior bona fide dwelling space – to avoid abuse of the concept.) The political division covers the citizens' political rights. And the family division covers dependents, primarily children, but also the aged and the handicapped; it deals with the various rights, responsibilities and powers necessary to maintain order in this sphere.

The economic rights authority deals with those spheres of primarily economic control which are essentially intangible yet have nevertheless evolved to the benefit of society. It has four divisions: an incorporation division; a contract division; a monopoly division, whose purview also includes intellectual property; and a currency division, which deals with money in the intangible state.

The mass communication authority deals with those spheres of control encompassing all the ways that we can or do communicate with each other on a mass scale. It has a separate division for every established channel of mass communication, as well as a division for emerging channels.

The spatial rights authority deals with all those spheres of control which describe the various ways we use space, whether that space be on or under land or water, or even in the air above. The largest division in this branch is the real estate division;

however, it should be noted and emphasized that this sphere of control is not absolute by any means, and should be understood to be limited to land access (including some degree of access control) and development. Often the spheres of control represented by the hunting division, the gathering division, the herding division, the farming division and the mineral extraction division will overlap with that of the real estate division and necessitate a coordinating of interests, access and usage. (In the past farming and herding, among others, have been implicitly part of real estate rights; but it would appear technology is transforming things enough that a differentiation should be conceptualized now, whether or not it is actualized as well.) The other divisions in this branch are the water-access and air-access divisions, dealing mostly with boat and aircraft use; and the fluvial-use division, which deals with surface water, groundwater and air, and is as concerned with controlling pollution as regulating water rights.

The property rights authority deals with all property that is not real estate and it is the smallest executive branch. It has only three divisions: an objects division; a vehicles division; and a money division, which covers money only when it is in a tangible state, cash, cheques, credit cards et cetera.

The societal rights authority is responsible for that overarching sphere of control which is the raison d'être of the state: the maintenance of security and order for society as a whole. The nature of this branch is performance within its sphere of control and it is useful to break this branch down into functions, each represented by a division. These functions include the armed forces (which encompass all aspects of border control as well as the military proper), the police, the diplomatic corps, the consular corps, state intelligence, health care, destitute care, education and the treasury.

Each branch head, as well as each division head, is appointed by parliament to a one-year term. Parliament has the power to dismiss and replace any head at any time. The one-year terms are renewable without limit.

THE JUDICIAL BRANCH

In many ways the judicial branch reflects the executive branches taken together. The judicial branch has one division for each executive branch, and each such judicial division is broken down into subdivisions in accordance with the respective executive branch's divisions. This is because the purpose of the judicial branch is to settle disputes arising out of the conduct of the citizens, corporate entities and the state as a whole in all their myriad interactions; and it can do this most effectively by having an organization essentially paralleling that of the executive branches, an organization that has already established the optimum context of dispute resolution by categorizing all conduct on the basis of the sphere of control it occurs in. In addition to these described divisions and subdivisions, the judiciary also has a steering division, as well as the supreme court over the entire judiciary.

The steering division contains the courts that decide in the first place which division(s) and subdivision(s) of the judiciary that any particular dispute will be resolved in. Every dispute will enter the judicial system via the lower courts of the steering division. These courts decide nothing other than the route the dispute will take in the courts.

Each of the seven divisions of the judiciary has lower courts, appeals courts and a superior court. While the intent is for there to be only three levels of court within a division, it is important that each higher court have a group of only about twenty courts feeding into it; thus, it will be necessary for some divisions to have an additional layer of courts, perhaps more than one additional layer. Technology allows us to get away from organizing the courts on a geographic basis; however, in certain kinds of disputes where live testimony is often critical, criminal cases for example, it is valid for the lower courts still to be organized geographically.

The role of the supreme court is to uphold the constitution. The supreme court monitors decisions all throughout the judiciary and steps in when it sees a decision not in accordance with the constitution. Normally it addresses only superior court decisions, but it can address ones from courts at lower levels too. A case cannot be appealed to the supreme court; it is the supreme court that must take the initiative. Besides addressing cases with an unconstitutional outcome, it is sensible for the supreme court to weigh in at times on cases with split decisions so as to provide closure and public confidence in the judiciary's interpretation of the constitution. There are twelve judges on the supreme court, nine of which are sitting. Each serves a twelve-year term. Supreme court judges are appointed by parliament, one per session; and parliament chooses from among three candidates nominated by the legislature. Only legislators may be nominated for the supreme court. The intent is that judges on the supreme court are fully conversant with the law and the constitution and the issues involved in composing legislation over the years prior to sitting on the high court.

A second task of the supreme court, or more precisely, of the three non-sitting supreme court judges, is oversight of the election commission. This task is critical to the proper functioning of the state. It is the one critical task that must be carefully isolated from the influence of the votive trunk, the body which in all other cases is seen as the direct source of legitimacy. Such isolation is necessary because of the nature of the election commission's task: the election of the incoming segment of the votive trunk. Without this isolation, the potential would exist for manipulation of elections or the perception of such manipulation. It is a lot to ask parliamentarians to completely set aside their own interests in the administration of elections. For the first nine years as a supreme court judge, the judge sits on the court; for the last three years, he sits on the election commission. This commission manages the elections start to finish each year, from enumeration all the way through the process until all the counts are made final and the candidates are elected.

MASS COMMUNICATION

The control sphere of mass communication, is fascinating. Modern technology, from Gutenberg on, has made it so enormous and all-pervasive that it has caught us completely off guard. We have yet to evolve socially even so far as to digest the printing press, not to mention photography, audio recording, video recording, cinema, radio, television, computers, video games and now the Internet. The impact each of these has on us by itself is mind-boggling; the impact of all of them added together – or, because of their interconnectedness, multiplied by each other – is of an order many magnitudes beyond that. How can one begin to quantify and categorize all of this? By form? By topic? By audience?

Perhaps the best place to start is at the definition of mass communication. What is mass communication? What is it that differentiates it from personal communication? Audience size, nothing less and nothing more. Personal communication has an audience of one, or some number quite close to one, whereas mass communication has an audience of no less than two and normally quite a few more. The channel of communication has considerable bearing on where – how close to two – this boundary is set. Some channels inherently limit audience size and so communication in them is generally perceived almost exclusively as personal. Face-to-face dialogue is one example of this, even when there may be four or five – or ten or twelve – participants. Television is just the opposite: even in a small community where at off-times it is quite possible that there is a total audience of only one (or none, for that matter), the fact that the potential audience is so much larger relegates this channel exclusively to the level of mass communication. So mass communication is distinguished from personal communication merely by audience size, and such demarcation is tempered by the channel of communication.

Exhaustively speaking, mass communication can be transmitted by visual, acoustic, tactile, olfactory or even gastronomic means – or any combination of the same. The bulk of mass communication, however, uses visual and/or acoustic means of transmission. Visual mass communication can come via two spatial dimensions (as in printing and painting), two spatial dimensions plus the temporal dimension (as in video), three spatial dimensions (as in sculpture and architecture) and three spatial dimensions plus the temporal dimension (as in live performance).

Visual mass communication of two spatial dimensions can be composed of two elements, text and graphics. Most of the channels representing this format originate in the publishing and advertising industries. They include books, periodicals, newspapers, greeting cards, artistic paintings, flyers, direct mail solicitations, display ads, product labelling and product packaging. The bulk of all this is produced on the printing press or its more advanced incarnations, but paint and other methods of surface coloration are used in certain channels.

Visual mass communication of two spatial dimensions plus the temporal dimension which is strictly visual describes silent video. This, however, is a very rare channel of mass communication. Far more – and overwhelmingly so – typical are the channels that combine the acoustic with this visual aspect. Included among these are cinema, television, audio video presentations and video games. Show business and the software industry are the sources of these channels.

Visual mass communication of three spatial dimensions often incorporates that of two spatial dimensions, whether text, graphics or both. It covers a diverse array of channels including artistic sculpture, architecture (where that is not strictly functional), landscaping (where viewing, rather than some more interactive use, is the primary purpose), display ads (from mannequins in store window displays to hot-air balloons floating in the sky), industrial design (particularly of consumer products) and product packaging.

Visual mass communication of three spatial dimensions plus the temporal dimension describes any type of live performance predicated on the presence of spectators. Unspectated sporting events are forms of leisure, exercise and competition: spectator sporting events are channels of live performance. Dancing among a crowd in a nightclub is a form of socialization and leisure; dance onstage is a channel of live performance. Acrobatics performed in private, whether in a gym, at a swimming pool, on a ski-hill or anyplace else, are forms of leisure and exercise; the same acrobatics done for an audience are channels of live performance. Adding in the acoustic aspect gives us the channels of in-person oratory, live drama and music in concert. So, besides the worlds of spectator sports and the performing arts, we have the realms of live entertainment, including everything from stand-up comedy to the circus; [live] political campaigning; [live] inspiration and enlightenment, whether religious or otherwise; and [live] education and instruction, when performed at the group level.

Acoustic mass communication, as noted, combines with visual to form numerous channels of mass communication. Where visual mass communication is absent and acoustic stands alone, we have the real-time channels such as those of radio and satellite broadcasting and the storage-based channels such as those employing vinyl records, magnetic-tape audiocassettes or optical CDs. The primary source for the content of these channels is the recording industry.

Although tactile, olfactory and gastronomic channels of mass communication are marginal, their existence should not be entirely overlooked. The scent of fresh baking consciously dispersed in its vicinity by a bakery is one such example. Other examples are product samples, whether edible (for the gastronomic channel) or otherwise (thus tapping into the tactile channel), and the source of virtually all such mass communication is the advertising industry.

It can be seen from perusing this brief survey what an enormous and diverse entity mass communication is. Nevertheless, many-tentacled though it may be, it is fundamentally homogeneous – rather than conglomerate – and therefore it is important that society, the state, approach it as a single whole. The piecemeal approach prevailing today, by contrast, not only permits inequities and imbalances among the various channels to arise, but also allows the reversal, to a considerable degree, of the basic command structure of society here so that, where it should be society controlling mass communication, in many ways we can see that it is mass communication controlling society.

What are society's interests regarding mass communication? Let's start by noting a miscellany of things that are not in society's interests. Encouraging people to overeat and overmedicate is clearly not in society's interests. Reducing people's inhibitions against breaking the law by glorifying lawlessness is clearly not in society's interests. Promoting the frivolous consumption of natural resources to the detriment of the environment is clearly not in society's interests. Entrenching the right to lie and deceive in the name of advertising and promotion is clearly not in society's interests. Transforming the citizenry, majestic and free, into merely another market commodity with a status just above that of domesticated animals is clearly not in society's interests. One could go on and on, the control sphere of mass communication is currently such a cesspool.

Society's interests regarding mass communication are that it serve as an effective network linking the minds comprising society; that it promote, rather than undermine, society's values; that it effectively balance the need for guiding thought, including inhibiting undesirable thought, with the need for nurturing creative thought, even to the extent of cultivating complete freedom of thought, abandonment of all inhibitions, within certain contexts; that it, the control sphere of mass communication as a whole, be well organized so that all of its constituent parts are properly focused on their rightful tasks and that all of these tasks are properly aligned so as to fulfill together their collective purpose; and that it always remain under the control of society as a whole rather than some small group or groups within society – or worse yet, any entity outside of society.

Perhaps the easiest way to understand society's interests regarding mass communication is to use the analogy of the brain: The brain is composed of numerous functions, whether macrostructural or microstructural, and they all must be networked together; the overall control function is what creates consciousness, and this function maintains control over the network. It is the same with society: mass communication is the network and our overall control structure, our government, must maintain control over this network so as to maintain control over all the other structures collectively comprising society. Moreover, just as some functions within the brain create thoughts that the overall control function chooses normally to suppress, so must some structures in society be permitted to generate ideas that society's overall control structure must normally suppress. Societal control over mass communication is crucial, but we must also maintain appropriate zones for creativity.

To organize societal control over mass communication we must first reduce it according to certain definable parameters. The most obvious of these is channel, which has already been described to a certain extent. Other parameters to consider include intent, intensity, duration, audience size, audience make-up, funding, transmission structure and energy use.

Intent of any mass communication will fall into one or more of three categories: entertainment, solicitation and education. The bulk of mass communication is entertainment of one form or another. Most show business models intersperse moments of solicitation to finance such entertainment, so that the bulk of such solicitation is commercial in nature. Other forms of solicitation are political, which waxes and wanes according to election cycles, and ideological, which includes religious. Mass communication of an educational nature includes instruction, such as in schools and universities; organization, such as occurs on the mass level at workplaces employing many workers; and information, such as is performed by news programs.

Mass communication of the highest intensity requires the focused attention of the recipient to the exclusion of other activity; paying attention thus, and possibly interacting too, is therefore the recipient's primary activity. Included at this level of intensity are things like book-reading and television-viewing. At the other end of the scale, mass communication of the lowest intensity requires only casual, or even subconscious, attention on the part of the recipient and causes no interruption of current activity. Examples of this include things like seeing a corporate logo on a building or hearing a radio commercial. Intensity of mass communication is a gradation ranging between these two extremes.

Duration of mass communication can be calculated in various ways. Perhaps the simplest is the most useful, and this is to find the time it takes for the average complete reception of the communication in question.

Audience size is straightforward. In many cases it may be necessary to use estimates, whether prior to or after transmission, in coming up with figures here. The optimal method of making such estimates should be found in each context and used. Note that the total audience over the full life of the communication should be calculated and, if necessary, broken down into analyzable sub-units. For instance, if a statue were erected in a public square then both the total audience size of its, say, three-hundred year expected lifespan should be calculated and sub-units of this total figure, broken down perhaps by year or decade, should also be given.

The main focus in ascertaining audience make-up is determining from there its sophistication. Communications aimed at relatively unsophisticated recipients, children for instance, clearly need to be held to more stringent standards in various ways than those aimed at sophisticated recipients.

Funding of mass communication ranges from fully consumer-driven to fully underwritten. When the full monetary cost of the communication is directly paid by the recipient, such as in buying a music CD, it falls in the category of the fully consumer-driven. On the other hand, when the recipient pays nothing directly (other than attention), and instead must merely endure being bombarded by solicitation at some level, the communication is fully under-written; examples of this include typical television programming and display ads like billboards. Intermediate forms of funding are also possible, for instance, movie previews shown prior to the start of a movie in a cinema or bought magazines that also contain advertising. Irrespective of its success or failure, the business model on which a mass communication is based determines its form of funding.

The transmission structure of a mass communication will fall into one (or more) of three categories: serial, parallel or asynchronous parallel. An example of a serial mass communication is the selling spiel an encyclopedia salesman may use on multiple residents in a neighborhood, one after another as he goes door to door. A program broadcast on television exemplifies parallel mass communication since thousands of viewers all watch it at the same time. And a downloadable video clip on the Internet typifies asynchronous parallel mass communication. When a television viewer records a program and then watches it later, this is an example of mass communication that is both parallel and asynchronous parallel.

However, unless there is considerable quantifiable representation in a secondary category, the primary intended transmission structure category of a mass communication should be used for quantification purposes.

Although today the energy expended in mass communication is invisible and goes entirely unnoticed, nonetheless there is waste here in vast quantities and it should be exposed – and done so routinely. For any mass communication all the energy used, first to produce it, second to transmit it and third to receive it, should be calculated. After analysis, figures should be given showing total production, total transmission and total reception as well as a grand total both in aggregate and broken down on a per capita (recipient) basis. In cases of bundled mass communication, for instance a television show containing commercials or a newsmagazine containing advertisements, the energy used for the separate communications should be calculated separately but then these separate calculations should be combined to reflect the combined communication predicated in the business model.

Besides the parameters given, there is one other fundamental element of mass communication that must be taken into account, and that is the division between content and distribution, a division that is sometimes vague. Although, precisely speaking, it is the content only that comprises the mass communication, and the distribution is merely its delivery (and means of delivery), even so, the relationship between the two is so intimate that trying to exert control over the one without also exerting control over the other would be hopeless. Therefore, in organizing and regulating the control sphere of mass communication, provision must be made for dealing not only with content, but also, where necessary, with distribution.

What should the organization and regulation of this sphere of control look like? The executive branch of government for mass communication should have a separate division for every channel of mass communication, as well as one to oversee emerging channels. All those entities, whether individual or corporate, who would be transmitters of mass communication should be licensed and activity in this sphere should then be restricted solely to such licensees. An integrated regulation code should be devised covering all aspects of the sphere exhaustively, both distribution and content in every one of its parameters. In devising this code, extensive consultation should be made with a broad array of industry representatives and watchdogs so that societal control here can be implemented effectively and all the tricks of this particularly devious trade can be confronted. A notable sea-change from current practice should be the imposition of high standards of accuracy and validity on all solicitative mass communication; this is justified because people inherently attach higher credibility to mass communication than to personal communication, and this is heightened further when such mass communication employs modern technology, anything from the printing press on. In addition to the administration personnel who will manage this sphere of control, a large corps of enforcement personnel will be needed. The more maximalist forms of mass communication will require ongoing scrutiny in line with the extent of the impact they have on society, whereas minimalist forms need not be subjected to such intensive governmental scrutiny but can instead be effectively policed by citizens facilitated in their efforts by streamlined processes of pursuing civil action against those out of compliance with the law. Furthermore, it is not unreasonable to demand submission of any mass communication of a potentially sensitive nature, news stories that could leak national secrets or reveal the identity of rape victims, for instance, to an oversight body for approval prior to transmission. (Needless to say, access to and use of mass communication should be denied to terrorists and others who would use it to try to manipulate or blackmail society.) Moreover, in return for some reasonable reduction in their licensing fees, providers of mass communication in certain channels, such as television, radio, newspapers and news magazines, should be required to establish, among other public services, substantial forums for political discourse and debate running for an appropriate period prior to each election and made available to all candidates at no cost so that society can eradicate, once and for all, paid political advertising from all channels of mass communication and thus remove the gross and anti-democratic distortions of the political process that the intervention of money makes there.

The control sphere of mass communication is fundamental to modern society. Although it is commonly perceived as primarily a platform for business activity and profit, such a view both ignores the interests of society as a whole and reduces individual citizens to mere commodities in the market. We must get our priorities straight here. The primary purpose and function of mass communication must be to serve as our collective nervous system, to connect us as individuals into the network that is our society; all other considerations, even the economic that today predominates, are secondary and peripheral. Restructuring this sphere will be an enormous and disruptive task, and may take many years to accomplish, but accomplish it we must.

MONOCULTURE, MONOCULT

There is no separating church and state. The state is the church. The thought system – the model of reality – on which the state is built is the state religion, the church, subservient to which must be all other thought systems present, whether referred to as philosophies, religions, ideologies or otherwise. Those thought systems which differ from the state religion accommodate themselves to it, whether through syncretism or through some form of supplemental compartmentalization; in either case they are appendages of the state religion, accepting it as their root. A differing thought system which fails to make such accommodation will meet with one of four results: eradication, expulsion, long drawn-out conflict, or triumph and emergence as the new state religion.

We moderns tend to have the misguided perception of religion as being something intentionally mystical. It may be true that many religions show a tendency to be stubbornly mystical, but this was seldom if ever the intent of their founders. In fact, just the opposite of mysticism and obfuscation has been the goal of each religion as it emerged. Rather than being the anti-sciences we view them as today, religions were the sciences of their times, each religion was the science of its day. The ancient agriculturalist with his fertility rites, no less than the nomadic warrior with his quasi-meteorological pantheon of gods, was interacting with his world in the way that made the most sense to his state of understanding. Look at Egypt and its incredible complex of personnel and time management necessary for the effective irrigation of the desert-bounded ribbon of cropland it depended on for survival: The system of thought which successfully performed this fundamental economic task was the state religion; and its body of practitioners correspond not to the clergy of today, but rather to our scientists. Egypt's state religion, scientific warts and all, was the science of its time and place.

One of the most useful things progress has given us is a demythologized perception of thought systems. What the masses of yesteryear had to accept on faith, and elevate accordingly, we are able to view with skepticism and evaluate in light of reason. We can see that religion, by whatever term we call it, is a macro-technology, one of the two macro-technologies upon which culture is based (language being the other). And we can tailor this macro-technology to align it with our progressively more clarified understanding of reality, rather than having to align our perception of reality to an ancestral understanding of reality expressed through the macro-technology. Thus, progress today proceeds along the more sustainable evolutionary path rather than the hit-and-miss revolutionary path it followed in the historic past.

The title of this essay is 'Monoculture, Monocult.' What is this monoculture, this monocult? Are there not thousands of cultures around the world? Are there not hundreds, if not thousands, of religions? No. There are not thousands of cultures around the world; there is only one, with thousands of subcultures. There are not hundreds of religions; there is only one, to which all others have submitted. (One could argue that Islam remains the lone hold-out; but that would be like saying the American Civil War did not end until Jesse James was laid low.)

To what country does the global telephone network not extend? Is there a people anywhere on the face of the earth yet untainted by the cotton/polyester blend? We need only glance at a world roadmap to see how ubiquitous the car has become. Corn, potatoes, wheat, steel, aluminum, air travel, television, radio, concrete, glass, McDonald's, Coca-cola, Visa: these are just a few of the evidences of the monoculture. A phone call is a phone call, whether in New York or Timbuktu, Paris or Papeete. On the other side of the coin we see that those cultural and religious practices which most blatantly offend the monocult, for example cannibalism, widow-burning and human sacrifice, have been eradicated, globally eradicated, and the writing is on the wall for various others offensive to a lesser degree. The monoculture predominates. Monocult rules.

Again, what is this monocult? We can see the monoculture; after comprehending the concept, it is simple to bring it into focus and see it anywhere – in fact, it is difficult not to see it everywhere. The monocult is a different matter. It has no creed to consult, no hierarchy to define its priesthood, no rites, no cathedrals, no prophets, no saints – nothing of the trappings or features we expect in a religion. Or has it? Perhaps in our familiarity with former religions we have come to expect a certain picture which no longer applies: robes, candles, rituals, chanting, the supernatural. Perhaps the monocult is so pervasive, so fundamental to our monoculture and now such a part of our very beings, that it hasn't even occurred to us to see it. Creeds? How about the UN charter, the Rights of Man, the US constitution – the very concept of charters, constitutions and bills of rights? There is your creed. The clergy? Lawyers, judges, politicians; there may be no overall hierarchy in form, but in fact there is, with the President of America occupying the same throne today which once held the likes of Churchill, Victoria and Louis XIV, and which eluded the unworthy grasp of both Napoleon and Hitler. Rites? Anthems, pledges of allegiance, awards ceremonies, platitude-filled speeches, national holidays: these, among other things, are our rites. Cathedrals? Manhattan is a cathedral, and the Ivy League schools are its cloisters. Prophets and saints? We have such an abundance, such a pool of luminaries to choose from depending on the need or desire: Locke, Newton, Franklin, Jefferson, Einstein, Nietzsche, Sartre,

BIOISM: THE DEITY OF LIFE

Voltaire, Rousseau, Descartes, Darwin, Paine, Marx, Shaw,
Shakespeare, Byron, Lawrence, Wilde, Edison, Roosevelt,
Wilson, Gandhi, Rockefeller, Hughes, Mao, Che, Lenin, Lennon,
Presley, Dean and Monroe, to name just a few. We even have
devils in Hitler and Stalin. The monocult is real; intangible
though it may be, it is as real as the British constitution.

Science, that vast body of illumination that provides so much
guidance throughout the monoculture, is a primary element of
the monocult; but it is not the monocult per se. The monocult is
deeper yet than science, for it is the foundation upon which
science was built. We tend to perceive the post-Renaissance
nation-states of Europe as antagonistic systems in competition;
however, the reality is that they have all along been merely
agents, often jousting for position, of the same system, the
monocult. Even the Cold War was a manifestation of such
jousting, two poles of the same underlying philosophy vying
against each other for dominance. International law, treaties and
conventions of warfare are entirely useless unless the parties
involved share the same fundamental system of thought.

The monocult is humanism, the elevation of man above all else,
the exultation of the corporate mind of man as the highest
available authority. Agnosticism and science are one result.
Democracy and the rule of law are another. The exultation of the
corporate mind of man as the highest available authority,

originally born in Greece and then reborn in Europe during the aptly-named Renaissance, has attained complete dominion throughout the entire world. The monocult is the undisputed world religion. Its highest objective, its highest ideal, is the furtherance of the human race, in all ways and at any price to the rest of biosity.

What is the relationship of bioism to this monocult, to humanism? Are the two synonymous, sharing a common outlook and common goals? No, although much of the basis of their thought is shared, there is also a critical divergence such that their goals and objectives are quite different. These are two systems of thought not in harmony with each other, but rather in competition. Does this mean that there will be a struggle between them before bioism prevails? Yes, it is only natural that some such struggle will occur. However, because of the nature of both – their mutual basis on and adherence to reason – it is not only a possibility but perhaps even a likelihood that this struggle will be maintained at the level of reason rather than sinking to something more physical. Let this then be our aim as bioists: to overwhelm and eclipse humanism – the monocult – through force of reason.

ECOCIDE

Ecocide is the great crime of our times and the greatest threat of all time to biosity. It is only now that we are beginning to recognize this. The hour is late, far later than is generally realized. We must act now. We must do a complete about-face and take responsibility for purging this globalized scourge from our terrestrial home. The cost will be great, but the danger is far greater. Every year we delay adds momentum to this freight train bearing down upon us all. Humanity, perhaps even biosity as a whole, is hanging in the balance depending on us to do our duty. We must confront and eliminate this Frankenstein of our own making, and we must do so now, starting this very minute. Ecocide must be brought to an end.

GARY WILSON

CONSCIOUSNESS OF CONSCIOUSNESS

Though we are animals, homo sapiens is unique within the kingdom. Like many of our lesser brethren, we are composed of flesh and bone. Yet we alone are distinct. Like all of them, we incarnate biosity: We eat; we mate; we live; we die. Yet there is that unbridgeable gulf between us and them, between our experience and theirs. What is it that makes us so very different? Is it our brains – these magnificent powerhouses of cognition? Perhaps, but the brains of our closest primate kin lack none of the components found in ours – only some of the capacity. What is it about us that makes us so special? – that sets us so far apart from the rest of biosity?

The person can be divided into two distinct parts: the body and the mind. The dividing point between these two is that boundary where the central nervous system ends and the peripheral nervous system begins. Therefore, the mind consists of the brain and spinal cord and all the rest is body.

The mind is composed of functions, some macrostructural and some microstructural. The macrostructures are things like the thalamus, hippocampus, amygdala, pons and cerebrum. They are pre-programmed to perform specific tasks, and the determination

117

of their full potential – which may or may not be reached in the course of development – is entirely genetic. The microstructures are neural patterns that contain information for use in specific situations. Some of these microstructures are pre-programmed, for example, the rooting and sucking reflexes in infants; whereas others, such as the ability to ride a bike or perform a mathematics calculation, are self-generated. All that said, to describe a living entity like the mind merely in terms of structure is woefully inadequate.

To get a full picture of the mind we must have, alongside functions, deliberation. Deliberation can be divided into two fairly distinct elements: conditioning and thought. Conditioning encompasses all the forms of microstructure self-generation that employ second-hand deliberation (that is to say, deliberation undertaken by preceding generations), and thus includes both classical and operant conditioning along with observational learning (but excludes learning gained through reasoning). Thought is deliberation at firsthand – that undertaken by the deliberator himself – and is comprised of imagination and will; the three products of thought are action, mere contemplation (which can be seen as action below the threshold where the boundary between the central and peripheral nervous systems is crossed) and microstructure generation.

Will is most apparent in thought's product of action, but it is also present in every other aspect of the mind: in self-generated microstructures (whether the product of thought or conditioning), in pre-programmed microstructures and in the macrostructures.

Considering the relationship of memory to microstructures, it becomes apparent that a valid model of memory is critical to understanding the mind. We are beginning to comprehend, to a slight extent anyway, the roles played vis-à-vis memory of macrostructures like the thalamus, hippocampus, amygdala and cerebrum, but what really is memory? And how does it work?

Let us begin by discarding the term "memory", condemning it for vagueness and relegating it to the realm of the vernacular. In its place let us use "sensor data storage" for the general sense and "sensor data track" for individual units of such storage, keeping in mind that any storage event will usually require storage for multiple sensors and therefore will require multiple tracks. "Sensor data storing" is the action of creating (or "laying down") sensor data tracks. All microstructures are sensor data storage containing one of two forms of sensor data: "pre-programmed sensor data", which is inherited, and "self-generated sensor data", which is not. While the actions of "sensor data location", "sensor data retrieval" and "sensor data collation" occur so instantaneously and naturally to us as to seem like one uninterrupted process, it is more useful to study and interpret them as the three (or more, for that matter) separate processes that they are. Both "recollection", which is sensor data location, retrieval and non-creative collation, and "extrapolation", which is sensor data location, retrieval and creative collation, are acts of the imagination. The centrality of the concept of "sensor data" throughout this exercise of defining memory can hardly be overlooked.

Sensor data storing involves neural (synaptic) changes. The laying down of a sensor data track involves changes to the whole series of neurons comprising that track. As noted earlier, any single storage event usually involves multiple sensors, thus multiple sensor data tracks. Since the tendency within the brain is for the sensor data tracks for each sensor (or sensor sub-group, for that matter) to be grouped together in one location, sensor data storing for a single storage event usually involves the laying of sensor data tracks in multiple locations throughout the brain: this is the parallel aspect of sensor data storing. Additionally, sensor data storing for each specific sensor within a storage event can involve the laying of multiple roughly identical sensor data tracks within the same location: this is the reiterative aspect. It becomes clear then, when you compound this reiterative aspect by the parallel, how widely spread throughout the brain the sensor data storage for a single storage event can be. It also becomes clear what an enormous number of sensor data tracks we are constantly laying down, day by day, hour by hour.

Sensor data storage capacity in the brain is finite; therefore, overwriting takes place routinely. After early childhood sensor data storing is entirely – or increasingly moreso – overwriting. However, the brain does not overwrite sensor data tracks haphazardly; rather, by design it seeks out those sensor data tracks within the target location which are among the oldest present there and overwrites them. How does it do this? There are two necessary processes: In the one a sensor data track – barring refreshment – is automatically "aged" in the tiniest of increments over a period of a few years until it is among the stalest tracks in its specific location and thus identifiable for overwriting; such "aging" is performed globally – thus, uniformly – throughout the brain by the hippocampus and involves neural changes so subtle and minute that they are detectable only in accumulation over time. In the other process, which works in conjunction with the sensor data storing process, sensor data tracks in a location are evaluated for staleness and accordingly selected for overwriting. So what we think of as "natural memory loss" – which is precisely that from the user's point of view – is, from the functional perspective of the brain, simply recycling, and particularly efficient and sensible recycling at that. This sensor data storage loss is gradual because the sensor data tracks for each specific storage event, being parallel times reiterative, are being overwritten not en masse but one by one with some variation in the cycling of the recycling cycle having occurred from location to location within the brain, the result being that recollection for a given storage event, were it to occur, would be potentially less and less vivid over time until finally every last sensor data track for the event has been overwritten.

Recollection and extrapolation affect sensor data storage in that their very occurrence serves to refresh the sensor data tracks drawn on. Since normally not all the involved tracks will be drawn on, this inserts an element of asynchronicity into the aging process for a group of tracks all stemming from the same storage event. Moreover, during the exercise of these two processes the imagination naturally generates bogus reiteratives with the result that the sensor data for the involved storage events is both further reinforced and simultaneously corrupted.

Sensor data tracks laid down at times of heightened emotion are taken by the brain as being of heightened importance and are enhanced accordingly. Neuromodulators are a key element of this enhancement process and they function here in two ways: They deepen the normal effects of the neural changes involved in the laying down of these tracks so that the duration of their aging process will be lengthened. And they attach markers to these tracks identifying them to the brain as candidates for later refreshment. Refreshment, a process whose tools are recollection and extrapolation, is performed subconsciously by the imagination and routinely occurs in the hours and days immediately following the laying down of a sensor data track. Dreaming is an important, and the most ostentatious, element of this process. While all sensor data tracks throughout the brain may be subject to later refreshment (there may be an element of randomness here due to the intertwined nature of sensor data tracks), it is those marked for such refreshment that are most likely to receive it. Procedural and declarative sensor data storage, which we as users differentiate between, are essentially similar in the brain's perspective and differ mainly due to the heightened emotion often present at the formation (and refreshment, for that matter) of the one and just as often absent at the formation of the other. (The other significant difference between the two is that the sensor data tracks of procedural sensor data storage are likely to be found in a great number of sensor locations throughout the brain, whereas those for declarative are likely to be limited to a small number of locations – and high usage locations at that, areas devoted to verbal, visual and auditory sensor data, where the cycling rate of the recycling cycle is highest in modern life.)

Sensor data tracks have been discussed here mostly as if they are discrete entities when in fact they are inextricably intertwined. Imagine taking a detailed roadmap of America and picking out a million different routes from New York to LA: every route may be unique but there must be extensive partial overlap so that some stretches of road appear in thousands upon thousands of the routes. The brain's neural network is something like that, but about a million times as complex. This does not change the essential validity of the model described here – statistics take the place of integers; it does add, however, an element of extreme complexity. Study of the brain, its neural patterns in particular, is thus incredibly difficult, and precision in such study all but unattainable.

Regarding sensor data storage, overwriting is not the simple replacement, track for track, of old for new; rather, it is the selection of that neural route which overall has reached the level of the stalest. This means that oddities such as ancient "ghost image" sensor data tracks are statistically not only possible but even routinely probable.

The model of memory given here addresses only long-term memory and has no relation to either short term or sensory memory, both of which are perhaps more properly understood in terms of some sort of sensor data comparison process. In any event it becomes clear that understanding sensor data storage is necessary in coming to an understanding of the brain's microstructures because all of them, even the ones that are pre-programmed, are masses of well-organized sensor data with switches based on such data interspersed throughout. So if we have gained a general understanding of sensor data storage, and subsequently of the brain's microstructures – for these are all nothing other than sensor data storage, then our comprehension of the mind is much more complete and we are able to approach the issue of personality.

It has been debated forever, but particularly over the course of the last century, whether personality is the product of "nature" or of "nurture". Though for many the debate still rages, research from the last few decades demonstrates clearly that personality is fundamentally genetic, that it is the product of the pre-programmed functions – both macrostructural and microstructural – within the brain. Self-generated microstructures, the result of conditioning and even thought, can have an impact on personality, but with important limitations. As an analogy, consider physique in two aspects, bone and muscle: Bone structure is an entirely genetic element of physique. There is an optimum form programmed genetically that will be attained in optimum conditions of development and the only effect intervention can have is negative. For example, look at the tribe in Africa where the women use a series of ring-like collars to lengthen their necks with the ultimate aim of making themselves more desirable to potential mates: in fact, rather than genuinely lengthening their necks, these women are crushing their shoulders and ribcages down toward their pelvises and so the appearance of lengthened necks comes at the price of overall skeletal damage.

Musculature, on the other hand, is not an entirely genetic element of physique. Genes decide the range of possible development, but it is left to environment to determine where within such range the point of optimum development may be located. With traditional societies whose cultures have been stable for many millennia, the San of Botswana being one good example, it should be fairly easy to say where within their range of possible muscle development is the optimum musculature. This is so because of natural selection's stabilizing influence. The monoculture, by displacing populations from traditional environments and mixing diverse populations, distorts this equation so much that immediate environment on the individual level is the primary determinant of optimum musculature and the genetic component is all but peripheral, inescapable though it may be.

Personality is like physique. Some aspects, as with bone structure, have genetically programmed optimum forms which will be attained in the optimum conditions of development and the only effect intervention can have on them is negative. (One must keep in mind, though, that just as the women who lengthen their necks derive a situational benefit from their own mutilation, so also in some cases there will be situational benefits rewarding those who have experienced specific forms of damage to their personalities.) Such aspects of personality are fully developed at birth or within a very few years thereof so that their "development" thereafter is not development per se but rather just maintenance. Other aspects of personality are more like musculature: instead of having genetically programmed optimum forms, they have genetically programmed ranges of possible development and the effect on them of intervention may be either positive or negative. When intervention – being microstructure development, whether through conditioning or thought – is in harmony with an affected aspect of personality, the effect is positive, and particularly so when a situational benefit is thus procured; but when intervention is in discord with the affected aspect of personality then dissonance results and the effect is negative. The optimum development of these aspects of personality equates to their full expression relative to the environment and immediate situation: what is an appropriate development for one time and place may be entirely inadequate for another. Conditioning and thought do not create any aspect of personality; their only effect is to channel the further development of existing aspects, whether positively or negatively, and their influence can be positive only on those aspects that, like musculature, are inherently malleable. Since such aspects of personality relate directly to environment and our interaction with it, then considering how human activity has outpaced evolution at such speed recently, it is to be expected that a common, perhaps even prevalent, phenomenon in today's world is considerable dissonance within the personality.

Related to personality and its development, but distinct from it, is the matter of masks. Not only are masks not part of personality, they are in fact the very opposite of it: masks are the concealment of personality. However, their development coincides in many ways with the development that personality undergoes. This is not to suggest that masks are harmful in and of themselves. They are actually very important socialization tools. It is only when they are fundamentally dissonant with the personality, or when they are permitted to hold sway over a person outside their proper and useful contexts, that their impact is negative. An extreme example of fundamental dissonance is the hypocrite, someone who gives lip service to one thing but practices just the opposite; and demonstrating a mask worn out of context could be a Grade One teacher who takes to interacting with adults as if they are young pupils. Properly used, masks serve as social interface tools regulating and standardizing communication and other forms of interaction person to person with the result that users and their objects mutually benefit. At the risk of taking the physique analogy too far, masks are to the personality what clothing (along with make-up and jewellery) is to the physique: anathema to the nudist but serving a purpose, to varying degrees of usefulness, for the rest of us.

We come now to the subconscious, that domain of magic and haunt of demons, the last refuge of madmen and mystics. Actually, the subconscious does not exist. It was just a mirage, merely one of the grand delusions of the twentieth century. It is true that various functions in the mind, whether macrostructural or microstructural, can perform subconsciously – even to the point of causing bodily action, including locomotion; but there is no global manifestation of personality in the person other than consciousness. There is no subconscious.

For consciousness to exist there must be a plurality of nonautonomous functions in the mind and one single control function – or integrated control structure – to manage them all: that is the phenomenon of consciousness. The state of consciousness, which is global, occurs when this control function or integrated control structure is active within the person. The state of unconsciousness, also global, occurs when it is inactive; and there is no global state of subconsciousness. So there is in the mind only one global phenomenon: consciousness; and two global states: consciousness and unconsciousness. While many functions within the mind can perform subconsciously whether the person is in the conscious or the unconscious state, without the phenomenon of consciousness all of the functions together would be nothing more than an amorphous mass either entirely directionless or at best subject to the single-minded direction of the most overpowering among them.

The keystone of personality is will, without which all is meaningless. The pre-programmed functions of the mind – the macrostructures and the pre-programmed microstructures – are those repositories of will within the person which combine to manifest personality. The other repositories of will within the person, those self-generated microstructures which are independent of the pre-programmed ones, do not contribute to personality; they are the source of masks. During consciousness, personality controls the person either independently or influenced by, and in conjunction with, masks. In either case the result is action, which is the ultimate embodiment of will.

Will is the one aspect of personality, of the person, which is, in the end, incomprehensible, irreducible. It is the aspect that keeps us from being mere automatons, that gives us being, that gives every living being, for that matter, its being. The existence of will leaves no room for the possibility of determinism and in fact validates the raising of metaphysical questions. This is not to endorse metaphysical interpretations of reality, any or all. The only correct and proper scientific stance regarding the metaphysical is one of uncompromising agnosticism. Nevertheless, it must be acknowledged that the fact of will facilitates metaphysical interpretations of reality.

So, to return to our original question, what is it that makes homo sapiens different from all other living things? What is it that makes us so special? – that sets us so far apart from the rest of biosity? The fact that we have brains does not make us unique:

species untold possess brains. Nor does the complexity of our brains: our closest relatives possess all the same physical elements of the brain that we possess. Nor yet does the fact that we have consciousness: animals galore have consciousness.

What sets homo sapiens so far apart from the rest of biosity is our consciousness of consciousness: While animals may possess consciousness, they are not conscious of such consciousness. We are. We alone among all the species of life on earth – which is to say, of all species of life known to exist in the entire universe – have both consciousness and the consciousness of it. This makes us very, very special indeed. We are unique. We have been unique ever since we became conscious of our consciousness, and that occurred following the development of abstract thought, which in turn occurred part and parcel with the development of language.

We have been considering homo sapiens here as an individual. Let us now complete this discussion by looking at him as the social animal that he is. Mankind has had consciousness on the societal level for eons. As long as we have had culture we have had such consciousness, for culture is that one integrated control structure which manages all the other functions that together transform individuals into a collective, a society. We are not unique in this because every society, human or animal, that has culture, even in its most rudimentary forms, has this consciousness on the societal level. Where we are unique here, just as on the individual level, is in our consciousness of such consciousness. We can pinpoint the exact genesis of this, for it occurred in historical times – or, to be more precise, it caused and accompanied the birth of history. I am talking about philosophy. Philosophy, discovered by the Greeks two and a half millennia ago, is mankind's consciousness of consciousness, that is to say, mankind collectively. Considered thus, philosophy is of incomparable importance to us. It distinguishes modern man from his predecessors. It is our tool for comprehending ourselves, for looking at the various functions within society – including the control function – and understanding how they interact and work together (or ought to work together). And, now that we have domesticated instinct and put it out to pasture, philosophy is the only reliable guide we have left to lead us into the unknown. It is at our peril then, as we have seen from the last century, an odyssey reeling from one catastrophe to the next, that we allow philosophy, our consciousness of consciousness, our tree of knowledge, to become overgrown with the choking vines of sophistry or subverted by the narrow perspective of any single branch of learning.

SEX PER CLINTON

"I never had sex with that woman!" Such was the claim of former President Clinton in reference to the young White House intern, Monica Lewinsky, a claim many – perhaps most – people considered to be an outright lie. Without wishing to cast anything but aspersions on the character of any politician – and particularly on one who is a lawyer to boot, I would like nevertheless to point out the possibility that in a narrow and correct sense Clinton was speaking accurately about his relations with Lewinsky. It all revolves around the question: What is sex?

At first glance it seems quite obvious what qualifies as sex: anything that leads to, or is meant to lead to, orgasm. A definition such as this matches the current popular usage of the word fairly well. Yet, in focusing solely on orgasm and employing it as the standard of evaluation, we are allowing ourselves to slip into a sensor-driven perspective on the matter rather than one that is strictly sensor-informed. To properly investigate the question, What is sex? we need to start by asking, "What is the purpose of sex?"

To some sex is the sacrament in a mystical union between two (or more) people; and this being, in their thinking, its purpose, their definition of sex proper will include that orgasmic activity that conforms to their perception of the sacrament and exclude any other as invalid. This is a demonstrably metaphysical point of view (aggregate of points of view, rather, as it covers quite a broad selection, many of which are mutually exclusive or otherwise opposed to each other) and therefore should be set aside as an invalid basis from which to proceed.

To some the only purpose of sex is the achievement of pleasure; in such a perspective sex is logically defined as any act leading to orgasm and is limited on the individual level only by preference and inhibition. This basis too must be set aside, as it is entirely sensor-driven, the expression of the sensophreniac.

The purpose of sex is no great mystery. Look at the animals (without anthropomorphicizing them). It's all about procreation, attaining a little genetic immortality. Orgasm is not the goal; it's the inducement. Bonding is fine, but that is entirely secondary to the production of offspring.

So where does this leave Clinton and his intern? The best evidence we have seems to indicate that the orgasmic activity involved between the two of them included oral stimulation, as well as various other forms of stimulation engaged in while the two of them were (or at least one of them was) fully clothed, but excluded vaginal penetration. If this is correct then the activity they actually engaged in could not, in and of itself, have led to procreation.

Assuming that Clinton chose to use the word "sex" in this strictly biocentric sense (while refraining from speculation as to his motive in arriving at such a rational usage at a time when the sensor-driven usage is far more prevalent in society), and that the evidence we have is accurate and substantially complete, then apart from one further clarification we should be ready to make a ruling as to his accuracy in the matter. This one clarification relates to the matter of orgasmic activity preliminary to procreative orgasmic activity: foreplay. Should foreplay be included in our definition of sex, in this biocentric definition of sex which Clinton presumably adheres to?

Foreplay, on the one hand, is not procreative in and of itself; yet, on the other hand, it does lead at times to procreation, even when the avoidance of the same was the conscious intent of the actors at the outset. So should foreplay, absent vaginal penetration, be included in our definition of sex? Inability of the actors to procreate together would be one clear limiting factor; but there is no reason to believe that this was the case here. If the actors are able to procreate together then it is a judgment call case-by-case as to whether foreplay should be regarded as sex per se: when the actors' intent is specifically non-procreative and there is no evidence that vaginal penetration has been achieved then it is generally fair to accept that their orgasmic activity could be maintained on a non-procreative level and therefore be excluded from the precise definition of sex.

Returning to Clinton and Lewinsky, the evidence overwhelmingly paints a picture of orgasmic activity very specifically non-procreative in intent and failing to reach the definitive threshold of vaginal penetration. Moreover, in Clinton we appear to have someone who has exhaustively proven himself capable of engaging in orgasmic activity maintained at a level below the procreative. So, even after taking into account the equivocal factor of foreplay, we are able to render the verdict that the preponderance of evidence vindicates Clinton in his claim that he never had sex with Lewinsky.

Clinton's words and stance in this matter clearly illuminate the bioist point of view regarding sex, whether that was his intention or not. Sex is procreative orgasmic activity; whereas non-procreative orgasmic activity is merely faux sex. Foreplay, that gray area seemingly between sex and faux sex, is actually sometimes one and sometimes the other; perhaps a term like "proto-sex" would be useful in describing it so as to encompass such ambiguity and ambivalence of potential.

THE MOTHERLESS SOCIETY

We are mammals. Motherhood is fundamental to our species. In fact, it defines us. Yet as a society we have allowed the role of motherhood to be relegated to a secondary status. Fifty years ago mothering was taken for granted as a woman's primary vocation while paid employment was viewed as optional and preferably avoided. Today paid employment is perceived as the primary vocation and mothering is seen as something optional to be fitted in with the least disruption possible to paid employment. This is a dangerous reversal of priorities, a necroferous development.

In the pursuit of equality and individual actualization, two worthy ideals, our society has tended in recent decades to blur the roles of the two sexes; or, to put it more bluntly, we have ignored, purposely and determinedly, the distinctness of the two roles. However, try as we might, we are unable to alter the reality: a man is no more capable today of being a mother than he was a century ago, nor a woman vice versa a father. That is simple biology. Further, despite the fact that a man is able to take on a variety of mothering functions, his brain is hardwired differently enough from the female brain that his performance of such functions is inherently less adept than that of a woman. What a man does outside his natural role with concentration,

137

effort and frequent incompetence, a woman does inside her natural role with intuitive fluidity and routine competence.

The problem here is not with the facts. Science can give us the facts. The problem arises when the facts and our ideals, or more precisely, our current implementation of our ideals, come into conflict. When we tie self-actualization to the career, instead of to mothering, we clearly put mothering at a perceptual disadvantage to a career. Far more importantly, in our materialistic society where economics is a recognized factor of equality, the single-income family is at a distinct disadvantage to the dual-income family, as is the non-gainfully employed woman to the gainfully employed woman; this disadvantage impacts offspring such that mothers in all good conscience are faced with the dilemma of pursuing paid employment for the benefit of their children, on the one hand, and on the other hand refusing to engage in paid employment, again for the benefit of their children.

Mothering is a generalist, multi-task role. These tasks can be grouped into two categories: instruction and the provision of care. During the earliest stages of a child's development the provision of care involves a fulltime mothering effort – more than a fulltime effort, in fact, if we define "fulltime" as forty hours per week. Many of these care tasks are tasks that, were we not viewing their performance in the mother/child context, we would associate with registered nurses and value accordingly. Similarly, many of the instruction tasks would be perceived to carry a far higher valuation were they to be found in a context other than that of the mother/child. Mothers are not viewed as language instructors, yet they are the heavy lifters in this particular transfer of technology, initially imparting speech patterns to their children via both monologues directed to them and conversation directed to others conducted in their presence, later conversing interactively with them, and still later using such interactive conversation to correct, refine and expand their grasp of language. If I today were to pick a language of which I have zero knowledge and then engage the services of a fluent teacher who would proceed to provide me a few years' worth of individualized and constant instruction, what would I end up paying? Or what if instead I wished to gain a firm grounding in the ethics of a culture unfamiliar to me, what would I pay for the similar services of a fully-trained ethicist? Language and ethics are just two examples from a myriad of technologies imparted by mothers to their children, and it is only familiarity that breeds in us the contempt – the gross under-valuation – of the motherly effort relative to the professional. (As a comparison of relative value, look at the quality of result in the area of language skills: how often is one's mother tongue fluency inferior to one's second language fluency?)

In discussing mothering solely in terms of mothers it is not to imply that the mothering tasks should be performed exclusively by mothers. It is appropriate that certain mothering tasks are shared between mothers and fathers, just as it is inevitable that persons other than mothers (and fathers) will also perform, or contribute toward the performance of, various mothering tasks. To some extent, having multiple contributors in the mothering process can be beneficial to children; however, it must be kept in mind that a mother (along with the father) is inherently the person with the greatest interest in the wellbeing of her offspring, and therefore the offspring's mothering is best provided, generally speaking, by her, the mother. Ideally, in the interests of the offspring, mothering is engaged in as the mother's primary focus. A working mother is disengaged to some degree, unless her work allows her to keep her offspring with her and prioritize mothering tasks over work-related tasks. Likewise, a non-working mother who employs a nanny is disengaged to whatever degree she allows the nanny to act as a buffer between her and her offspring.

Non-maternal mothering comes in two forms, vicarious and surrogate. Vicarious mothering is mothering performed essentially the same as the mother herself would perform it, and thus is almost always undertaken by relatives of the mother, these being people who have learned mothering skills from the same source; examples of vicarious mothering providers would include a child's older siblings, cousins, grandparents, aunts and uncles. Surrogate mothering differs from vicarious mothering in that it is merely the replacement of a mother's own mothering with mothering presumably equivalent in effect but not necessarily in process. Surrogate mothering may be a neutral phenomenon in the provision of a child's care; but in the area of instruction it is highly invasive of territory that a mother (a parent) ought to maintain in her own control. Much of that part of a child's character that comes from nurture rather than nature is the product of all the various forms of instruction inherent in mothering. The mother who surrenders her child to surrogates surrenders the formation of his character, for good or ill, to people who could never inherently care for his wellbeing and success as much as she does or ought to.

Returning to the overall problem, the de-prioritization that mothering has undergone in recent decades, there is a solution. First we must remove the economic disadvantage entailed in a woman's opting for mothering over paid employment, and secondly we must remove the widespread perception that mothering involves the abnegation of self and suppression of one's pursuit of self-actualization. The surest way to attain these ends is to professionalize mothering, and by that I mean recognizing it as a genuine vocation, salarizing it, and instituting training and standards (within reason) for its performance. The big issue here is salary – money. Where shall the money come from to provide equitable salaries to that proportion of the population, say ten percent, actively engaged in mothering young children and currently receiving no salary for such activity? There are two sources for these funds: the fathers of the children, and society as a whole as represented by government. In the case of fathers, we already have a precedent in divorce situations of the ongoing transfer of funds for the children's upkeep. This transfer of funds into the mother's control should be standard in all situations a mother finds herself in, whether that be marriage, divorce or unwed motherhood, because control of the purse strings is a significant power no matter how benevolently it is wielded. (Note that in the context of marriage this discussion relates solely to motherhood, as distinct from wifehood.)

While few would question fathers' responsibilities for their own children, some might wonder where the justification is for society having to chip in as well. The fact is that society, although made up of individuals, is itself an organism and as such its first and foremost task is its own perpetuation; since mothering is society's natural mechanism of perpetuation, if it allows mothering as an institution to wither away then society will be condemning itself to wither away as well. Society already recognizes this as evidenced by government programs such as children's allowance, child tax credits and the baby bonus. Moreover, society also already funds surrogate mothering via means of daycare, kindergarten and primary school. The proposal here is to take all these various funds and pay them directly to a professionalized motherhood in the form of regularized salaries, re-organizing the affected societal structures accordingly. A further source of government funds could come from appropriate government jobs set aside specifically for engaged mothers, whether allowing for the presence at work of their children or providing them light or flexible schedules tailored around their mothering tasks; jobs created in the various new organizations involved in the professionalization of motherhood would certainly be excellent candidates for such treatment. Ultimately the idea is to collect all the different funds and combine them into a single salary for each mother, calculating each according to all the criteria involved. If the resulting dollar amounts reflect a substandard rate of pay then society will have to bite the bullet and fork over more funding, establishing both a minimum salary and a respectable industry median salary.

As to instituting professional training and standards for mothering, please keep in mind the stated qualifier of "within reason": No attempt should be made to deny motherhood to any woman. The purpose, rather, is to quantify the multitude of tasks within the mothering role, identify the preferred methodologies for each of these and then disseminate the resulting standardized knowledge to mothers and those studying to become mothers; this is particularly important in that elements of standardization inherent in the early years of public education will now be the responsibility of mothers rather than teachers. An incidental result of this program will be the elevation in the popular perspective of mothering, its professionalization in the public perception. Additionally, a network of cooperatives should be established to assist mothers to perform certain mothering functions as part of small-group efforts the way home-schoolers today collaborate on various aspects of their children's education. These cooperatives should incorporate considerable flexibility to allow mothers a fair degree of control over the choice of groups they participate in. Properly established, this network of cooperatives will provide four benefits: it will allow for various efficiencies inherent in group effort such as specialization of function and concentration of undertaking; it will reduce the loneliness of mothering that has arisen in our increasingly insular urbanized society where much of the mothering role is performed in the isolation of the single-family dwelling; similarly to reducing the mothers' loneliness, it will reduce the children's loneliness and afford them the important development aspect of socialization; and it will establish the context for accountability in numerous mothering functions, the basis of both the professionalization of motherhood and the public perception of such professionalization.

There are numerous complexities in this matter and no pretence is being made here that implementing this proposal will be either quick or easy. For instance, how should we determine the extent of funding to be provided by the fathers? Guidelines will have to be established, but clearly such determination must be made on a case-by-case basis. The same is true for determining the government's contribution; factors such as degree of maternal training and development, number and age(s) of children, and extra input within small-group efforts, among numerous others, should all have a bearing. In the interests of the children it should be the policy to promote the most stable homes possible; yet this policy should not be pursued in a way that ends up penalizing children who have the disadvantage of living in unstable homes. In the interests of society the desired rate of population growth (or reduction) should be determined and reflected in the factor of salary relating to number of children, so that the government is not inducing an undesirable rate of population change. These are just a few examples of the complexities involved; there are multitudes of factors to be considered in such a large and complex undertaking as this, many of which are not yet apparent. By maintaining ourselves in a learning mode and keeping our focus at all times on the objective of the perpetuation – and indeed the robustness – of our society, we will be able to accomplish what needs to be done. The intent here is not to turn the clock back a century and relegate women to a subordinate role in society relative to men, discarding our ideals of equality and self-actualization in the process. These ideals are worthy and desirable. The aim, rather, is the transformation of our implementation of them such that women can participate fully in their pursuit without having to fight their own biology and its imperatives. This is every bit as much in the interests of women individually as it is in those of society collectively. The alternative, on the societal level, is decline and even eventual extinction; for the de-prioritization of motherhood is learned like any other attitude and can be expected to become more fully internalized and effectuated with each passing generation. We must, as a society, recognize this danger and reverse the process, if it's not already too late. The motherless society is a society on the brink of extinction.

INFANT MORTALITY

With the noblest and most compassionate of motives, modern man has sought to eradicate infant mortality. This undertaking, which has marched from victory unto victory unto victory over the past century or so, which has met with such astonishing and overwhelming success on virtually all fronts, is one of the most short-sighted and disastrous blunders yet committed by our species.

The three basic causes of infant mortality are disease, malnutrition and injury. What happens when we combat some type of disease and thereby reduce the infant mortality associated with it? The individuals saved have in effect been ransomed, and this ransom comes in the form of the robustness, to some degree, of their health. Such a trade is beneficial to the individual, who lives only one lifespan, but harmful to society with its greater longevity and subsequent need for uncompromised robustness. For example, let's say the infant mortality rate from Disease A is 10%: if we combat this disease effectively in a population for one generation then the robustness of 10% of that generation is compromised. At 10% this is relatively insignificant. Let's say now that we do the same for four generations: not only is there the cumulative effect of the 10% directly compromised in each generation, but now also there is the compounding effect of the compromised individuals breeding with the uncompromised and passing on their compromised robustness to some percentage of their offspring. Thus, after four generations it is not just 40% of the population that has compromised robustness, but perhaps upward of 90%. So what happens if the disease morphs and we are left unable to combat it? There will be a correction. The bigger the bubble we have created, the bigger the correction. The worst-case scenario is the extinction of the population. The factor of genetic mixing between the compromised and the uncompromised makes this possible, even if unlikely.

When we consider infant mortality caused by disease we are actually addressing a host of discrete phenomena because each disease is generally a separate and distinct entity. The same is not true for infant mortality caused by malnutrition. Virtually all cases of this are due to environmental factors, or more specifically, ecosystem overload. As with disease, intervention here – apart from suitable relocation – benefits the individual to the detriment of the society. The critical factor in this case is not robustness though, but rather sustainability. However, the underlying issue is still natural selection. Whereas natural selection uses disease to winnow out those with a susceptible genetic make-up, it in effect uses starvation to reduce a population whose faulty decision-making has put it into an environment that cannot sustain long-term the numbers it has reached. Most forms of intervention are detrimental to the society long-term because they necessitate an increased strain on an already vulnerable and overloaded ecosystem. For instance, consider the use of well water for irrigation in an arid climate: The water table in this environment is likely such that farming is viable only in floodplains, so that whatever population this can support is the sustainable population. By using well water for irrigation, though, it is found that the arable land can be increased by a factor of ten, thus the population. However, eventually the wells begin to go dry. For a while this can be compensated for by deepening the wells, but soon even that does not suffice. At this point catastrophe strikes and natural selection reduces the population to its sustainable level, lower now than it originally had been with its pristine water table. The use of well water was the bubble factor, and the deepening of the wells was the magnifier. The individuals living in those generations of successful irrigation benefitted from that practice, but overall the society incurred harm from it. Moreover, in light of the aspect of genetic immortality, even the original beneficiaries were ultimately harmed in that the vast majority of their descendants in a subsequent generation died in the correction. On careful consideration, would anyone want to contribute to a die-off of 90% of their posterity a few generations down the road?

If it is fair to say that natural selection uses starvation to address faulty decision-making on the societal level, then it is similarly fair to say that it uses injury to address faulty decision-making on the individual level. For instance, there is a good reason we – and I believe all primates – have an innate fear of snakes and spiders: those individuals in our distant ancestry who had such fear avoided these perils while their fearless brothers did not and were slowly winnowed out of the gene pool over the generations – or eons. That is just one example. The critical factor here, as with disease, is robustness, but mental in form now rather than physical. Since it revolves around decision-making, this "mental robustness" should be understood to involve determination along with intelligence, and both in whatever amount is sufficient on an incident-by-incident basis.

When one considers all the types of disease, all the forms of injury, and all the causes of ecosystem overload that contribute, individually and in combination, to infant mortality, one can see what a complex mechanism it is. Where there is no intervention, it culls the majority of infants. To demonstrate this, let us assume a stable population with a pre-industrial culture: This means that the average woman reaching sexual maturity will produce exactly one daughter who will reach sexual maturity. How many live female births will it take to produce this one mature daughter? If the average woman survives for fifteen child-bearing years then it is reasonable to assume that she will produce six live offspring, half of whom are female. This scenario suggests a natural infant mortality rate of 67%, which is likely reasonably accurate. (This particularly in light of the fact that infant mortality is the continuation of a culling process that began at conception, and in the prenatal phase of this process the fate of two out of every three fertilized eggs, on account of chromosomal defects and other factors, is eventual spontaneous abortion.) So in reducing this rate to virtually nil we are introducing a massive distortion, a multitude of distortions, into the natural scheme of things. For every contributing factor of infant mortality that we have brought under control, we have created a bubble, and all of these bubbles together comprise a super-bubble. If this situation were ultimately sustainable then there would be no cause for concern; instead of interpreting these developments as distortions, bubbles waiting to be burst, we could see them as part and parcel of human evolution. However, few or none of these developments are sustainable; genetic defects and faulty decision-making, whether on the individual or societal level, structurally weaken the species and necessitate an ongoing and growing intervention for their continued tolerance. The result is inevitable: there will be a day of reckoning and the longer we put it off the more drastic it will be. Every intervention we make is an insulation of our offspring from reality, from the natural order. In aggregate we are isolating humanity from the rest of biosity, we are retooling ourselves as an island society. The problem with this course is that island societies and other such isolates tend to become evolutionary backwaters and subsequently vulnerable. Look at the various native species of Madagascar and New Zealand: how many of them have become extinct since the arrival on their shores of mankind? Or look at what smallpox alone did to the indigenous population of the Americas in the centuries following 1492. Harsh as it may sound, it is far better for us to take our medicine (in a manner of speaking) and tolerate infant mortality, to watch two out of every three of our children die before reaching adulthood, than to gravely weaken our posterity and subject it to an eventual correction which in any event will be cataclysmically disruptive and which can only be greater in severity the longer it is delayed.

How realistic is it to expect parents to sit quietly by and watch their children die without lifting a finger to save them? Completely unrealistic. Even if they understood the importance of that to the wellbeing, perhaps the very survival, paradoxically, of their posterity, I doubt that they could restrain the urge to render assistance. Children are real; posterity is just an abstraction. This is not to suggest that we are without remedy here. There are things that we can reasonably expect parents to do, things which are at least partial remedies. And there are other things that we can expect society to do. In the fight against disease it is primarily society that creates the distortions because it is society, and not individual parents, which has developed and provides the various vaccinations and inoculations used to combat or eradicate the different diseases. Unlike individuals, society does have the long-term interest, thus the foresight and fortitude, to make the difficult decision to terminate programs like these which on further reflection are found to be antithetical to the wellbeing of our posterity. Society has the ability both to terminate these programs and to make private resort to such medicines socially unacceptable. The ball is also in society's court in matters involving faulty decision-making on the societal level. Where individual parents are most responsible for providing remedies is in the area of faulty decision-making on the individual level. Here as well we can expect nothing other than that parents will do their best to protect their children and will never sit idly by when danger approaches. However, there are ways of protecting children which inherently strengthen them and leave them prepared to deal with problems on their own, and there are ways of protecting them which merely insulate them from harm and subsequently leave them just as weak and vulnerable as they had previously been. It is the former that we must foster and encourage parents to adopt – and while this means identifying and learning innumerable specific behaviors, it also means more fundamentally taking on the mindset in accordance with our objectives here.

Despite all our victories in the fight against infant mortality, we are enlisted in a losing cause and we must make a strategic retreat – and that on many fronts. This is an enormous task I am proposing. It will require a lot of research and analysis, as well as a lot of tough decisions. It may be many, many decades before we succeed in this, but succeed we must because we are badly over-extended and vulnerable to correction – massive correction – unless and until we do. For those who object and say that we must not play God, I can only respond that I could hardly agree more: We have been playing God here for a century or more and we must now stop.

ESCAPISM

Is reality so awful that we should all want to escape it? Everywhere I look today in Western society it seems that I am seeing escapism. Consider television: What is network primetime filled with? Sitcoms, where laughter is often so manufactured that the viewer must be cued by a studio audience to produce it at the appropriate points. Dramas, filled with idealized and homogenized people and events supported by effects designed to awe, rather than enlighten, the viewer. Sports, where tiny elites engaged in meaningless competitions beckon the viewer to live vicariously through their heroics. And above all, commercials, where drinking a fizzy drink made from water, sugar and a few chemical compounds for looks and taste will put you on top of the world: where buying and addicting yourself to some new pill will have you rejuvenated and ready to lark on the beach of your dreams; and where the next episode of what-have-you will be even more of an unforgettable must-see than was last week's episode.

Network primetime television is just one example of the pervasive escapism of today. Alcoholism is escapist, the flight from reality into the mind-numbing arms of self-medication; likewise drug abuse. Pornography is escapist: ecstasy-craving

losers attempting to overcome their inadequacy via means of
visual stimuli instead of the real thing. Faux sex is escapist:
people searching for meaning to their lives at the level of the
physical sensor rather than the deeper biological process that
such sensor is intended to trigger. Consumerism in general
exhibits an overwhelming degree of escapism: the momentary
enjoyment of a fast-food meal meant to appeal to your palate
with little regard for your overall wellbeing; the fleeting pleasure
of a trip to some sun-washed paradise whose inhabitants would
give their eyeteeth to switch citizenships with you; the extended
indulgence in a new car whose condition and functionality all but
mirror those of the three-year-old model you traded in for it, and
whose novelty wears off in a matter of weeks, if not days; to cite
just a few instances. Pulp fiction is escapist, the immersion in
some well-worn model of reality adapted by an author to appeal
to that faceless market segment that is his audience, helping
them to pass a little time away in a state of waking somnolence.
The word "pastime" and the whole concept it represents is
inherently escapist, whether or not its various manifestations are
entirely so. Most mysticism is escapist, be that the Muslim
baffled by modernity and responding with jihad; the Catholic
who manages to attend mass a couple times a year, listening to
words that pass immediately from his mind, then bowing his
head and shutting his eyes while more words drone by; the
Scientologist who deludes himself with science fiction; the
Buddhist whose nirvana is the final leaving behind of

consciousness, of being; and so on and so on. Even many participatory sports have a considerable element of escapism to them: an urbanite five hundred miles from home gliding down snowy mountain slopes on waxed sticks of fiberglass; a couple college students using racquets to hammer a little ball around inside a closed box the size of a classroom; an adult repeatedly climbing a ten-foot ladder only to leap from the board or platform at the top into a tank of water below. Everywhere today, I see escapism.

It is true that escapism is pervasive in modern society. Yet it is also true that many things which have a strong escapist element, many of the things listed above as exemplifying escapism, are not entirely escapist, or are not necessarily always escapist. One critical factor is equilibrium: For instance, alcohol in an undistilled form such as beer or wine, if consumed in moderation, will not produce a mind-numbing effect and can even be beneficial, rather than detrimental, to one's health; used thus, its consumption clearly is not a demonstration of escapism on the user's part. Pulp fiction, the enjoyment of which normally manifests escapism in the case of a mature adult reader, can to some extent be material employed as a broadening exercise for a juvenile reader who is building his vocabulary and grammatical skills through even such substandard means. And, to consider the issue of equilibrium from the opposite end of things, something generally so bioferous as weight-lifting, for example, can often be observed to develop into a passion substantially escapist in essence with its partakers pursuing disproportionate muscle gain for their physiques or entirely overbulking them without regard for any target physique that would be optimally functional for their current or desired lifestyles. The factor of equilibrium is fundamental to the understanding and evaluation of most forms of escapism.

Along with equilibrium, the other main factor in considering whether or not – or to what degree – a pursuit is escapist is intent. Watching television to view a sporting event is almost certainly escapist in intent; whereas, watching television to catch an episode of a nature show and expand your knowledge of reality is anything but escapist – until, of course, you catch yourself taping and replaying the scenes in which the lions kill the hyenas, and cheering the lions on, over and over again. Playing a video game to blow away or hack apart every living thing in sight is little other than escapism, and depraved escapism at that; but playing a video game to come to grips with another person's model of reality, and to pit your wits and strategizing skills against what opposition exists within that model of reality, can be a valid learning experience rather than an exercise in escapism – just as long as the equilibrium factor does not kick in adversely. There are even forms of pure escapism the discovery of which and exploratory encounters with which are not necessarily escapist in and of themselves:

BIOISM: THE DEITY OF LIFE

Though Aldous Huxley ingested various mind-bending drugs in his experimentation with them and investigation of their properties, it is clear that his intent, if not his methodology, was essentially scientific, rather than escapist, and his book detailing his experiences is well-respected in that light. So the factor of intent should never be overlooked in evaluating escapism: one man's escapist pursuit may just be another man's genuine learning experience.

A pertinent question at this point is: What is not escapist? On both the bestial and the sapient levels of life the two fundamental objectives are survival and the exertion of will. However, whereas the scope of beasts' means in pursuing these objectives is limited to the development and maintenance of abilities and capacities, the expansion or maintenance of control – be that over space and matter or fellow entities, and self-propagation through procreation, homo sapiens has expanded his scope to include the conscious exploration of reality, along with more abstract forms of self-propagation than simple procreation, in addition to the more primal means in his pursuit of survival and the exertion of his will. We can say then, that a person's actions are not escapist when he is developing or maintaining abilities or capacities that further his survival or the exertion of his will; when he is expanding or maintaining some form of control over territory, things and/or people that furthers his survival or the exertion of his will; when he is self-propagating, whether through the straightforward means of procreation, the abstract means of monument creation, or even perhaps the unconfirmed abstract means of metaphysical immortality, such that his posthumous survival or exertion of will is furthered; or when he is consciously exploring reality, increasing his knowledge of reality, so as to further his survival or the exertion of his will. Interestingly enough, in contemplating escapism, or more precisely, in defining what actions are not escapist, we incidentally confront, via such negative image, purpose, the issue of human purpose. The above enumeration of actions not escapist can be taken as a comprehensive picture of human purpose. Now let's look at a couple aspects of this picture in a little more detail.

Monument creation is a very broad designation. A mausoleum is a monument memorializing a deceased individual, immortalizing him (however briefly and incompletely) in the minds of others. A book is a monument memorializing the author's thoughts before and after his death; thus it provides him some measure of immortality. A philosophy is a monument, whether to an individual and his thoughts or to a group and their collective output of thought – and as far as one's abstract survival and posthumous exertion of will are concerned, this may be the most complete form of immortalization possible. In addition, there are innumerable other forms of monument: a business, a movie, a government policy, an estate, a public work, a town, a painting, a sculpture, a temple et cetera. You get the idea.

The conscious exploration of reality is performed by each individual in two different ways: through the direct study of reality itself, and through the study of other persons' models of reality. All of us use both of these methods for exploring reality. The curiosity of a child leads him into endless direct investigations of reality: the plucking and eating of a bright red berry to see if it tastes good, the squishing of a beetle to see what happens, the unwrapping of a gift to find out what's inside. It also leads him into endless verbal investigation of other persons' models of reality: Why is the sky blue? What happens when you squish a beetle? When do we get to Grandma's? The exploration of reality through studying other persons' models of reality also describes education. It would be nice if every single one of us could directly and independently explore all facets of reality so that we could be entirely confident, and self-sufficiently so, in our knowledge of it; but such a wish is not realistic. Reality is too huge for any individual to tackle all of it directly on his own. Hence, education. This is the sharing of models of reality by those who have directly studied the facets of reality in question with those who do not so directly study them – or who directly study them much less completely, but instead rely on the accuracy of the models being shared. As long as education is based on valid models of reality, it is an excellent way for individuals to increase their knowledge of reality; but when the models taught are wrong and misleading, such as that old one that said the earth was flat, or that older one that said the sun was drawn across the sky each day in a chariot pulled by horses, it is questionable whether their propagation does more harm or good to the learner. At any rate, it should be kept in mind that increasing one's knowledge of reality must be pursued for the purpose of furthering one's survival or the exertion of one's will; otherwise even such a respected activity as this sinks to the level of escapism.

What are we to think of escapism? Obviously, it has so far been presented here in quite a negative light. But is such a negative view of it warranted? Is escapism really all that necroferous a phenomenon, or is it more in the order of a harmless distraction? The answer, quite simply, is that escapism in and of itself is necroferous to the individual. It distracts the biocentric, to whatever degree, great or slight, from his biocentrism; this is necroferous. It occupies and consumes that precious and irreplaceable commodity, time; this also is necroferous. And in some extremes it causes its victims to deplete their resources and neglect their health and social standing; such degradation of one's overall wellbeing is the most patently necroferous effect of all. (This may be a good point at which to note that relaxation, in its proper place and proportion, should not be confused with escapism per se – so let's not drive ourselves to throw the baby out with the bathwater here!)

Whereas escapism is clearly necroferous on the individual level, an interesting and ironic thing is that in some cases it seems to have a positive outcome at the group level. For instance, an obsession with video games is necroferous for an individual, but that same obsession, on the national and global level, has been a significant factor in the continuing development of computer processing power. Is this to say then, that escapism can be harnessed for bioferous ends? That it should be so harnessed? Or rather, should we focus on the lost potential involved in such vast multitudes of people devoting time to silly obsessions like video games, time that perhaps could be employed in ways ten times as bioferous? These last two are difficult questions. On the one hand, it feels inconsistent to promote any form of necroferosity or benefit from the same, whether on the individual or the societal level; yet on the other hand, it seems wasteful and therefore unwise to stand on principle and refuse a benefit derived from the necroferous actions of those who are freely exercising their wills in applying themselves to escapist pursuits. Ultimately, the goal is for every individual to be entirely biocentric, leaving escapism behind for good. Currently, few if any of us are thus, and it will likely be many generations before humanity reaches such a serene state. As long as we keep this goal in mind, though, and pursue it faithfully, we should be able to pick a path – perhaps each of us his own different path – without erring either to the one side, compromising our ideals, or to the other, turning ourselves into rigid and intolerant ideologues.

Western society today approaches escapism differently than do other societies, and differently even than it itself has done in previous eras. We in the West now live in a very permissive society. In a lot of ways this is a good thing. Freedom is not a meaningless ideal, praises of it empty platitudes. The exertion of will is a fundamental objective of life. Total freedom is equivalent to the entirely unfettered exertion of will; therefore, any dilution of freedom is a restraint upon the exertion of will. As far as the area of escapism is concerned, this means that society's best course is to refrain from placing any restrictions whatsoever on the conduct of legally competent individuals so long as the activities they engage in cause harm to nobody apart from themselves. To quite an extent this is indeed the course we follow; however, there are a couple glaring exceptions to our policy of permissiveness: recreational drug use and remunerative sexual activity – and these exceptions, these inconsistencies, demonstrate clearly the futility of interventionism.

Recreational drug use has filled the prison systems across North America to where they are currently bursting at the seams. If you were to release all those inmates convicted of drug possession or trafficking, along with all those convicted of internecine crimes stemming from the unregulated nature of an outlawed industry, in addition to those convicted of property or other crimes committed with the primary intent of financing drug habits and those convicted of crimes committed while under the influence of drugs, you would reduce the prison population continent-wide to about a quarter of its present size. In the context of a legalized recreational drug use industry, each of these four categories of crime would be virtually eradicated: possession and trafficking are crimes that in most instances are created inherently by the fact of illegalization; internecine crimes within an illicit, thus unregulated, industry demonstrate more the innate chaos of a power vacuum with no established authority than any essential criminality of orientation; when the cost of a highly addictive substance is no longer a thousand times higher on the streets of America than in the fields of Bolivia – a hyper-inflation due solely to government intervention, the financing of drug habits will cease to be a pervasive criminal problem; and when recreational drug use is permitted with adequate controls for the protection of society in general, the incidence of crimes committed by people under the influence of drugs will drop dramatically. We are shooting ourselves in the foot here with this futile prohibitionist drug policy. The population that is accordingly incarcerated, being in the range of one half of one percent, is almost entirely male and working-age, thus equivalent to well over one percent of gross domestic profit. The high cost of incarceration is another serious hit to gross domestic profit, as are the costs of law enforcement, prosecution and the enormous burden on valuable court time. Overall, the damage to the gross domestic profit from this vain frontal assault on recreational drug use must surely be in the range of three percent annually, year after year, if not higher – and this doesn't even begin to consider the psychological and collateral damage incurred by such a confrontational approach.

Like recreational drug use, remunerative sexual activity – prostitution – under normal circumstances harms nobody apart from the wilful participants themselves. Many people see prostitutes as vamps, but the fact of the entirely unregulated nature of the illicit industry in which they work means that they are more often victims, victims of both the pimps who exploit them and – in corrupt jurisdictions – the police who exploit both them themselves, for pleasure, and their pimps, for protection money. The incarceration figures here don't come anywhere near to those resulting from the fight against recreational drug use, but the total is still a fair number of people, mostly women. And what are we guarding? Public morality? Morality is obviously no longer an issue, in reality if not in perception. The only real danger that we should be addressing in this matter is the spread of disease; and that can be controlled far more effectively – as can prostitute abuse – through a legalized and well-regulated industry than through useless attempts at outright prohibition.

Let's step back now and examine the qualifier "legally competent". As applied to individuals, this excludes those not of sound mind; but more importantly, it excludes children as well, those individuals who have not yet reached the age of legal competence. It is right that society refrain from fettering an individual's exertion of will so long as such exertion causes harm to nobody apart from that individual himself; it is also right that society recognize that children's wills are still in the formative process, vulnerable to suggestion, and must be protected accordingly, permitted to grow and develop in an environment free from necroferosity, in this case the necroferosity of escapism. And here is one of the great failings of our society, of the indiscriminate permissiveness of our society. It is true that we are conscious of our responsibility here, that we do seek to insulate children from the more obvious forms of escapism such as pornography, tobacco, alcohol and drugs; the only problem is that our performance in this is next to useless. What child can't get his hands on a dirty magazine? Or a pack of cigarettes? Or alcohol, or drugs? These last two illustrate clearly both the inadequacy of current control mechanisms and the futility, in even this respect, of outright prohibition for the adult segment of society, neither of which methods shields children as desired. Worst of all, our performance to date in these matters works, if anything, to tease and titillate children, thus increasing the very desires we mean to discourage and forestall. While it is true that our performance here is a problem, it is more a symptom of a deeper problem, the genuine problem: we have allowed escapism to take a higher priority than the wellbeing of our children. If you doubt this, take a look at television some Saturday morning – and don't even worry about the programming (an issue in itself), but focus instead on the commercials: On the one side of the equation you have highly-paid, well-experienced, professional advertisers with enormous advertising budgets; and on the other side sits gullible little six-year-old Joey, the easiest target in the world for the message that true happiness comes from possessing the latest toy, eating the sugariest cereal, watching the coolest new show. Laissez-faire is, generally-speaking, a good stance – but is it serving us well in this instance? In assigning control of segments of the airwave spectrum, should we not ensure that such control is not harnessed for the exploitation of our children? This is only one example of how we allow escapism to take a higher priority than the interests of our children. The solution to this problem is not to fix one thing here, another there. The solution lies in re-evaluating our priorities and re-orienting society accordingly, from the bottom on up. This sounds difficult and extremely disruptive, but in the long run a paradigm shift is far easier and more satisfying to implement – and, ultimately, far more effective – than an ongoing piecemeal approach that is little more than putting out brushfires.

Children need to be protected from exposure to influences that are beyond their developing abilities to cope with. This suggests some degree of sequestration from the tentacles of escapism, and

I accept that as valid where reasonably implementable. It also suggests a strong emphasis, from even an early age, on education, parental or other, designed to reveal the necroferosity of the various forms of escapism – and escapism in general – to children so that they are able to meet these sirens, when the time comes, on a footing of equality, rather than the inequality of near-helpless victimization evident today. This is not to advocate the regimentation of childhood or the eradication of play (which, in fact, can be seen all throughout the animal kingdom in the development of the young and their skills), but rather the preparation of our young so that they can attain their own complete development and be able to fully exert their own wills untainted by necroferous influences.

Again, is reality so awful that we should all want to escape it? No, of course not. First of all, the fact of mass media today exposes us to levels of perfection – personal beauty, for instance – far higher than are natural in everyday life. As long as we keep from allowing such exposure to distort our own standards and expectations, we should manage just fine with this. Secondly, we are living in an incredibly rich society increasingly divorced from nature. There is great danger here, but I am confident that a resort to philosophy will be the foundation of an adequate defence. And thirdly, metaphysics injects an element of confusion into the whole exercise – and we don't even know if there is anything there. My personal response to metaphysics is simply an appeal to the imagery of football: You've got to catch the ball before you start running with it; otherwise you are liable to get distracted and drop the ball without even catching it. Life is catching the ball, and when that's done then you can think about running with it. (Which is not to imply, though, that parents do not have the right – moreover, the responsibility – to impart to their children their own [possibly escapist] metaphysical beliefs.)

No, reality is not so awful. We just have to be realistic about it.

[Author's note: Although this essay contains important and valid ideas, it is disjointed and unfocussed. I intend to revise and restructure it extensively, likely breaking it into two or more essays. September 2013.]

RITUAL AND TABOO

Ritual is a manifestation of conditioning. Without conditioning there could be no ritual. Ritual is not a spontaneous event; rather, it is a deliberately created event. Ritual is the child of deliberation.

When, in response to a call to prayer, a Moslem faces toward Mecca and prays, it's not as if he has spontaneously formulated a decision to pray right then and there. That Moslem is acting out of habit and such habit stems from the deliberation of his spiritual forebears, meaning ultimately Mohammed and whatever even earlier sources of deliberation influenced him in his founding of Islam. When a Jewish family celebrates a son's entry into manhood, it's not as if they have suddenly observed his attainment to maturity and spontaneously decided to celebrate the fact; they are acting out of habit, habit passed down generation to generation and reflecting both the deliberation of the originator and that of all those intervening participants who added their own modifications. And when a group of Christians gathers on December 25 to exchange gifts and sing carols commemorating the birth of Jesus, it's not as if they have just up and decided to celebrate the nativity of their Lord; they are acting out of centuries-old habit born of the deliberations of all those, Christian or otherwise, who contributed elements, knowingly or not, to the present form of the commemoration. These are just three of innumerable examples of ritual to be found in the world of religion.

Disregarding, rather than discounting, any possible metaphysical dimension to ritual, we can see the social significance of practices such as prayer, praise and the celebration of holy days. Prayer on the individual level is effective for focusing one's thoughts and aspirations, summoning encouragement in the face of difficulty or adversity, building confidence in spite of incomplete knowledge or understanding, and orienting oneself to a group's outlook so as to bond with that group. Prayer on the group level is similarly effective as on the individual, yet with a heightened element of group bonding; additionally, group prayer is a vehicle for communicating thoughts and attitudes – and not just their communicating, but their guiding as well. Much the same can be said of praise as of prayer; however, praise is generally more physical and less verbal than prayer, and therefore its theatre is more the emotions than systematic thought. Holy days, whether on the annual level such as the Fourth of July or Bastille Day, or on the weekly such as the Jewish Sabbath, are effective vehicles for group bonding and orientation of thought. The weekly holy day, occurring so frequently and constantly, is particularly effective and may in fact be the primary factor in both the survival of the Jewish culture post-dispersion and the growth of Christianity and Islam.

Another body of ritual with social significance is that focused on the life cycle: birth, adulthood, marriage and death. The most important of these is marriage ritual. By delineating spousal and parental relationships and the subsequent structures of control within society, which is the basis for a considerable portion of law, marriage establishes a viable context for procreation and child-rearing. Marriage predicates society on biology; it is parenthood ritual prior (normally) to the actual attainment of the parenthood. Birth ritual, whether christening, circumcision, baby dedication, birth certification or what-have-you, serves to introduce a new member to his society and afford the group the opportunity to become aware of and accept him; though the child understands nothing of the goings-on, he is being attached to the group officially for all within (and without, for that matter) to know. Birth ritual is, in a sense, a form of societal procreation. A second form of societal procreation is adulthood attainment ritual: while this parallels most aspects of birth ritual, now the new member is perceived as a free and responsible agent, able to act – and acting – wilfully. The previously alluded to bar-mitzvah is a clear example of this ritual. Another good example, though more of a group entry ritual than simply adulthood attainment, is baptism as practiced among numerous Protestant denominations. Less obvious but still valid examples are driver's license acquisition, citizenship ceremonies, graduation ceremonies, the initial exercise of one's right to vote after reaching voting age and a first carouse after reaching legal drinking age. The final and concluding ritual in the life cycle is death ritual. It is second in legal significance only to marriage for it entails the re-assignment of control in various contexts. Wakes and funerals are one element of death ritual; by providing an opportunity for group recognition of the decedent's passing, they offer an outlet for mourning and closure as well as an occasion for bonding and regrouping. The probate process, to whatever degree of sophistication, is the other element. The death of a farmer without a will a few centuries back would perhaps have resulted, apart from the death tax, in the simple transfer of his land and livestock to his eldest son or the division of his estate between all his sons. Nowadays a similar passing would likely result in a prolonged legal negotiation, if not struggle, leading to a complicated division of assets and likely requiring some degree of liquidation. Most people today exert control in a variety of spheres; when death occurs, all of the involved spheres of control will be affected and will experience re-adjustment of some sort or other. The probate process addresses this re-adjustment and seeks to control it to a reasonable extent; though it seems de-ritualized, it is no less a part of death ritual than a marriage contract or pre-nuptial agreement is part of marriage ritual.

The one other area of ritual with a widespread impact originated with an entirely agricultural orientation and focused on events like solstices and equinoxes, planting and harvesting. Easter may be celebrated as a religious occasion today, but it originated as a fertility festival and was later adapted to a Christian use. Thanksgiving began as a specific commemoration stemming from a specific event experienced by the Mayflower pilgrims, but it took wing because, in coming to represent the harvest festival, it resonated deep within the popular psyche. Agriculture fixed the annual cycle in human consciousness and paved the way for the creation of a host of annual ritual events, from the impersonal New Year's Day and Labor Day to the highly personalized birthday and wedding anniversary celebrations. Such events attach meaning, deliberately created meaning, to otherwise indistinct days.

Ritual is one group manifestation of conditioning. Another is taboo. Ritual and taboo are intimately related; they are like two sides of the same coin, one positive and the other negative. Ritual has something to posit, whereas the intent of taboo is to negate.

Taboo is the group refusal to entertain consideration of, or otherwise countenance, a given activity, and thus represents the group's utter condemnation of such activity. Taboo is a form of condemnation derived from conditioning rather than from any immediate logic. (And, ironically, most of the widespread condemnation of it today derives from conditioning rather than from any immediate logic.) This is not to say that, as a phenomenon, taboo is spontaneous. Like ritual, taboo is the child of deliberation; it is a deliberately created phenomenon, whether forming in an instant of reaction or growing slowly over untold generations. Taboo is the recognition that most human activity is not reflexive, but flows from thought; that an activity which is not sanctioned or nurtured in the imagination is unlikely to occur. Taboo is the recognition that imagination is the engine of humanity.

A prime example of the power of this engine is the copycat crime. The contemplation of crime is [hopefully] not normal and generally subsists well beneath the surface – beneath the active level – of human consciousness (due, it might be noted, to taboo). An exception to this is when a dramatic crime occurs and receives considerable public attention. Suddenly, for a short while that crime takes on a potentiality that it did not previously have in people's minds and, for a few, enters, even if only briefly, the realm of possibility. If it occurs that such a crime is susceptible to imitation then all the ingredients are present for a wave of copycat crime. The significant element here is the substantiveness of the catalyst acting on the minds of the copycats. Violence encountered in movies, novels and video games certainly exerts some power of suggestion over people's imaginations, however slight; but violence observed in reality, even though seen through the filter of the media, has considerably more substantiveness than that ingested through fiction and therefore exerts a far stronger power of suggestion. The imagination may be prone to flights of fancy, but only from the realm of reality – what it perceives to be reality – will it derive choices to present to the will. This engine of humanity, the imagination, is what taboo seeks to govern.

The division of the person into body and mind is a useful perception. So also are the divisions of the mind into functions and deliberation; deliberation into conditioning and thought; and thought into imagination and will. The circle is complete with the linkage between will and body, for nothing we do, not even the thinking of the most fleeting thought, is done apart from the means of the body, our interface between will and action. (True, will is present in conditioning, functions and body; however, it is increasingly programmed and autonomous, relative to the imagination, in each of these aspects of the person. To illustrate, with some effort you can contravene your conditioning (assuming that you are honest) and tell a lie; with considerable determination you can suppress your drive to consume food, or even to ingest liquid; but no exertion of conscious willpower will allow you to overrule your body and stop the beating of your heart.)

Of the above divisions, the most pertinent to the discussion of ritual and taboo is conditioning. Whereas thought is deliberation at firsthand, thus immediate to the deliberator, conditioning is second-hand deliberation incorporated by – rather than immediate to – the deliberator. Put another way, conditioning is deliberation undertaken by preceding generations and imparted to the recipient who incorporates such on the basis of his faith in the source and thus with little or no deliberation on his own part. Conditioning, therefore, is a form of immortality: ethotic immortality, the immortality of the ethos.

The word "conditioning" is something of a misnomer because, looking at it in terms of parent and child, it predicates the parent as actor and reduces the child to an object to be worked on. The fact is that the child is the actor and the parent, contrary to appearances, is merely an object, the object of the child's observation. This is so because a child is capable of rejecting conditioning or choosing that of one source over another – children do have wills of their own, after all. It is true, however, that in this case of parent and child the parent has the power to direct and limit the child's exposure to sources of conditioning and so is not an entirely passive participant. The keys to conditioning are exposure and observation.

Just as a parent uses direction and limitation of a child's exposure to guide and influence the child's conditioning, so society uses ritual and taboo to guide and influence the conditioning of its members. Ritual is society's directive form of conditioning; it is used to direct members into specific channels of desired thought and conduct. Taboo is society's restrictive form of conditioning; it is used to limit members from specific and general channels of objectionable thought and conduct.

What are we to think of ritual and taboo? At first glance they seem an offense to freedom of will, not to mention simply backward. They are certainly among the first targets of any revolution. Yet, by the same token, revolutions inevitably engender their own tailored forms of ritual and taboo. As Solomon said, and Orwell more recently reinforced: There is nothing new under the sun. Half a century ago obscenities were verboten, but today they are okay. Does this mean that freedom of speech has triumphed over taboo in the matter of vocabulary? Try, if you are a teacher, exposing a classroom of students to the term "niggardly" and see what happens to your career. Taboo is not overcome and extinct; it has just migrated to new pastures. It seems more than likely that ritual and taboo will always be with us.

Trying to banish ritual and taboo is pointless. Instead we must recognize them for the important and useful social tools they are and use them in the best way, the most bioferous way, possible. Moreover, we need to humble ourselves and accept the fact that in many cases rituals and taboos represent much deeper and broader perspectives than our own as individuals. They are evolutionary; they have developed often slowly and incrementally over scores and hundreds of generations, thus allowing for the maintenance of their more viable incarnations and aspects and the withering away of their less. This is not to make a blanket endorsement of existing or recently abolished rituals and taboos; rather, it is to caution against hasty condemnations of them from narrow points of view. The sexual revolution taking hold in the '60s seemed like such a good and liberating thing at the time, but who today can ignore the plethora of unintended and unwelcome side effects following in its wake? Those forms of ritual and taboo most widespread throughout the cultures of the world are the ones we should take most seriously of all and be the most wary of uprooting, for their embodiment of human wisdom and experience is profoundly holistic.

Ritual and taboo are useful social tools, but they are more than that: as forms of conditioning, ritual and taboo are society's means of attaining ethotic immortality. Just as parents, through conditioning their children, realize this form of immortality to some degree, so we as a society gain some measure of the same through the conditioning of incoming members. With this in mind, it becomes clear that however significant the immediate effect may be on us ourselves of our rituals and taboos, far more significant is their long-term impact on the development, flourishing and evolution of our posterity in the coming centuries and millennia. Therefore, hand in hand with an attitude of reserve toward innovation, we must have a willingness to optimize such conditioning as this in light of technological progress and the ramifications it has for society.

Our aim should be to acknowledge ritual and taboo as the powerful tools they are and maintain them in good repair, harmonizing them and our perception of reality together. The more complex modern life becomes, the more need we have for them, the more need we have, that is, for the capability they offer us of transferring decision-making from thought to conditioning – from immediate deliberation to incorporated deliberation – so as to preserve thought, our thought function comprising imagination and will, from becoming overloaded. Whatever rituals and taboos we decide to maintain or create, it is crucial that they be in harmony with and manifest, however directly or indirectly, the underlying model of reality to which we adhere. Moreover, as a body they ought to exhibit a completeness and balance relative to it so that the scope of their applicability has no predetermined limitations – meaning that, whether or not posterity chooses to apply ritual or taboo to any given aspect of life, the option is always there within a rational context. As long as it is backed by reason and such backing – in the form of fully enunciated explanations – is available at some level to its recipients, conditioning in the form of ritual and taboo, and our employment of it, need not dismay us in any way whatsoever.

PHILOGENESIS

"Philogenesis" is the love of beginnings and it can be taken to encompass such on many different levels. It is the curiosity one has about the early lives of one's parents, along with the lives of one's grandparents and other immediate ancestors. It is the fascination one has with the history of one's own people, whether political, cultural, social or otherwise. It is the delving into the ancient cultures from which sprang one's own, whether genetically, ethotically or both. It is the study of the evolutionary record that leads ultimately to the rise of mankind. And it is even the analysis of the cosmos, the cradle of our existence, in search of an explanation for its having come into being. All of this is philogenesis.

Why is philogenesis important? That is to ask, why are the various forms of philogenesis each and of themselves important, and why is philogenesis as a whole important? Philogenesis as a whole is important because it addresses the question of identity; its various forms are important individually because addressing such a complex, multi-faceted question cannot be done with any simple, independent response, but instead requires a multi-pronged approach that is a process of learning. Moreover, philogenesis is important because it allows us intellectually to contextualize our mortality, to make peace with the inevitable.

Ultimately there is linkage between these two issues, identity and mortality, and for almost all of known history they have been the exclusive domain of the metaphysicists. What seeming inroads humanism, with its exultation of the individual, has made on identity have come at the expense of its position on mortality. Humanism, so overwhelming in virtually all other matters, has more than met its match in death, from which it can and does do nothing but shrink back in helpless terror.

Philogenesis, then, is important – critical – to the bioist because it provides the basis for a rationally defensible position on these two unavoidable issues that have always been the playthings of the metaphysicists. This is not to say that we can produce full answers here, as the various systems of metaphysics purport to do. We cannot. However, we can demonstrate a perspective that is consistent with the facts available to us and that is adequate in providing individuals both a sense of belonging in life and one of peace in time of death. Furthermore, with recourse both to the facts and now to their proper interpretation, we can wrestle from the metaphysicists their primacy – the primacy of their formulations – in these issues, and thus discredit all the false promises and delusions that have been propagated. Just as biosity allows us to maintain integrity while addressing the issue of purpose, so philogenesis allows us to do the same vis-a-vis identity and mortality.

GARY WILSON

URBANITIS

Urban populations are not sustainably self-replenishing. This may sound incorrect, and dramatically so, in light of the recent rise of vast cities all around the globe. Yet it is true, it has been true all throughout history, and it remains true today. The populations of cities do not replenish themselves; instead, they are replenished by their hinterlands – until their hinterlands run dry.

Why are urban populations not sustainably self-replenishing? Focus. The urbanite has lost focus; he has lost touch with biosity. He does not hunt for his daily nourishment, nor does he gather it from bushes and trees. Neither does he raise stock or, for the most part, even grow a vegetable garden. He has thus lost that day-in-day-out contact with the rhythms of life that naturally serves to maintain him as a biocentric. Is it any wonder that the urbanite is an escapist? That he spends most of his time in escapist pursuits? Having lost his biocentricity, he has become estranged from the purpose of life, something best grasped through the daily performance of activities involving nature. The failure of urban populations to self-replenish vividly demonstrates such purposelessness.

The ironic thing is that necroferosity of this nature on the individual level should lead to bioferosity on the collective level, and such exceeding bioferosity at that. Yet it does. Urbanization – civilization – has produced enormous advances in knowledge and our ability as humans to extend our range and habitat. Assuming we do not over-extend ourselves to the point of global habitat destruction (something that is not presently a safe assumption), urbanization in all its individual necroferosity will have proven to be one of the most bioferous tools yet devised by mankind. That said, the price paid for this tool has been high, perhaps too high. We have paid for urbanization by instalments through the gradual domestication of our species. The urbanite is at the vanguard of this trend and he is now all but domesticated. The average city-dweller, were he to be cast away into any but the most benign of natural environments and forced into a stance of total self-reliance sans technology, would likely survive for a period of time little longer than that representing the internal consumption of his own store of body fat – and that discounts the possibility of his demise due to dehydration, hypothermia, disease, injury, accident or animal attack.

So what are we going to do? Abandon the cities? Turn our backs on technology? Go back to nature? Not likely. What we need to do, instead of that, is find a way whereby we retain the advantages of urbanization yet at the same time revive our innate biocentricity. Although our goal here is essentially a mental restructuring of ourselves, to accomplish this we must first undertake a physical restructuring of our cities. We must do this to admit biosity back into our lives. The following is an eclectic assortment of suggestions toward this end. They are not comprehensive, but rather are meant as a starting-point.

Personal water use in North American cities is prodigal. Did our grandparents waste water as we do? No. Having to pump your water by hand from a well and carry it into your home naturally regulates usage and deters excess. Likewise having to heat your water on a stove. We have allowed our enjoyment of convenience here to grow into a curse. We need to re-learn old hygiene habits whereby small amounts of water replace our bubble baths and extended showers. Except for the elderly and the handicapped, we need to remove our bathtubs altogether. We all need to adopt water-saver devices or models for showers, toilets, washers and dishwashers. We need to remove all private swimming pools. We need to quit washing sidewalks with water. We need to quit watering all merely ornamental greenery, whether lawns, shrubs or trees. Restricting our soap and detergent usage to that which is the most environmentally friendly is also important. And if we can re-introduce some sustainable form of natural regulation, we should.

Current traffic management is a mess, and growing worse almost everywhere. Modern technology, in the form of vehicle roboticization, will offer solutions to many problems here. The enormous driving efficiencies available to robotic vehicles (convoying being just one small example) will reduce infrastructure overload. Routine, even daily, cab use will become viable so that private ownership of vehicles will decline, and along with it the need for widespread and extensive parking facilities, whether on public streets or in private garages. Most residential streets can then be made one-way only and narrowed, allowing for more green space. Concentration of vehicle ownership will allow for the rapid and efficient introduction of anti-pollution technology and practices. And between the freeing up of space and the improved safety of our streets, we will be able to re-design our cities into walking-friendly environments.

Our community life is a wasteland. When we aren't in our inward-oriented homes or our fenced yards we are speeding from garage to destination in our closed vehicles. It's no wonder that our neighbors are strangers. The car is a major culprit here in that it has broadened, massively, our options in interaction and friendship, options that we have exercised to the full. Yet, industrialization in general, with its economies of scale and division of labor, is the fundamental cause of our collective alienation. We bus our children to progressively larger and more distant citizen factories where they are strictly segregated by age. We retire our elderly and deposit them in summer camps for the aged where they can best be nursed into the great unknown away from our squeamishness of the same – out of sight and out of mind. For every good or service we need we have some specific set of anonymities to turn to, whether in person or by phone. While one cannot help but appreciate many of the efficiencies represented here, there are at least three areas where a slight sacrifice in efficiency will be rewarded by a large restoration of community. The first of these is schooling: progressive education, which has given us so many excellent reforms, has also saddled us with the dreadful, anti-communitarian organization we have today. We must replace this organization with what we formerly had: the one-room schoolhouse in the very immediate neighborhood where all children, from Grades One to Nine or so, mix and learn together. This can be done without sacrificing quality or uniformity of education because we now have the important tool that is the Internet.

The second area for consideration is our treatment of the elderly: not only does their segregation harm them, it harms the rest of society too in that we lose the benefit – and our appreciation – of their knowledge and wisdom, and not only of their knowledge and wisdom, but also of the daily exhibition of their love and concern for society. We need to make a conscious effort to return to the old ways of doing things here where each one of us makes a priority of taking his aging parents – and other relatives, when the need arises – into his own home and caring for them there; and if we can reinforce this action through government policy relating to taxation or inheritance, then so much the better. (Moreover, we need to eradicate forever the very concept of retirement.)

The third area for consideration here is the grocery store: this is the one consumer destination that is so constantly frequented that it is quite arguably an integral part of the community. As a society, we should take advantage of this, rather than merely trusting the invisible hand of the market for the most beneficial outcome. For the sale of all perishable goods, we should replace the mega-store with a series of smaller outlets strategically placed so that most homes are within easy walking distance of one. We should require that a trained nutritionist be on duty at each such outlet during store hours. And we should ensure that the goods are as uniform as possible, whether in price or condition, from store to store so that there is no incentive to shop anywhere other than the nearest store (as far as selection is concerned, just-in-time technology and constant replenishment can be depended on to tailor each outlet's offerings to the local market). Such a network of grocery stores will not only contribute to a revitalization of community feeling, but it will also improve urban life through the facilitation of numerous healthy habits and practices.

The way we use urban space today is abysmal. Virtually all of our green space is ornamental. Such ornamentation is positive psychologically and contributes to improved air quality, but is otherwise of little comparative value. We can gain these same benefits from more practical greenery, along with many additional benefits. Not to deny anyone the pleasure of a flower garden, but everyone should have, as their first priority, a vegetable garden, the bigger, the better. We should embrace all the practices of the organic gardener, from composting to sun-drying and everything in between. Lawnmowers should be abolished and their role taken over by livestock. Pesticides and herbicides should be outlawed, and our intolerance of anything other than weed-free homogenization overcome. The trees and shrubs that we introduce should be fruit-bearing, for the most part. The size of the average yard should be increased significantly. And the raising of small livestock, even up to the size of sheep and goats, should be encouraged.

The last issue that I will raise here is the dwelling. There are so many ways that we have gone wrong with this. We use ever-increasing amounts of ever-more-synthetic materials to create ever larger spaces for ever fewer occupants – all of which must then be lit and heated (or air-conditioned, as the case may be). Do we need so much space? Privacy easily grows into isolation. Are we better off today than our ancestors in their crowded little dens, their cozy little micro-communities? Be that as it may, we need to limit the synthetic and flammable materials used in our dwellings; we need to raise the occupancy to square footage ratio; and we need to be far more efficient than we are with lighting and insulation so as to reduce energy usage. These are a starting-point.

Urbanization is a critical stage in human evolution. It is something we have yet to master, as is evident by the collapse of all civilizations preceding our own and the rapidly falling birthrates everywhere throughout the monoculture. The intent of the proposed strategies is not the rejection of urbanization, but rather its salvation in a sustainable form through a process of partial re-ruralization. In restoring the biocentricity of the urbanite, we will put urbanization on a sound footing once and for all.

MACRO-CASHFLOW INDEX

Confidence is the currency of any currency. Where confidence in a currency disappears, so too does its value. This was as true when gold or silver was the medium of exchange as it is today in an era of paper money and electronic transfers.

There are two kinds of confidence that people have in a currency. The first is based on knowledge of what goods or services can reasonably be expected to be obtained in exchange for a certain amount of the currency in question. This is always necessary, and in fact so crucial that producers of currency will go to great lengths to nurture such confidence. The minting of coins originated with the need for specific units of [precious metal] currency that its users could trust to be the correct amount. Subsequently, laws introducing severe penalties for the debasing of coinage were enacted to counter such activity as it arose and shook users' confidence in the full value of the coins embodying their currency. In modern times debasement has evolved into counterfeiting and it is confronted aggressively by the producers of currency through ever more elaborate methods of both printing bills and apprehending counterfeiters. Besides such an ostentatious threat as that, modern producers of currency must deal effectively with many other factors, some internal, others external, which could result in the erosion of confidence in their currencies if left unchecked, things like inflation, government debt and trade imbalances.

The second kind of confidence that people have in a currency can be equated to their recognition of the value of prior enterprise expressed as confidence in the value of future enterprise. This is not individual enterprise, but rather collective societal enterprise. Confidence in such enterprise is necessary for the successful development of any floating currency. In that context it is the intangible value underwriting the more tangible value manifested in the first kind of confidence. In essence, what this second kind of confidence is saying is that, based on its recognition of the value of a society's enterprise in the past, it expects that society's future enterprise similarly to be valuable so that, in turn, their currency too will maintain its value.

Because confidence is the foundation of any currency, and the only entity in any modern economy big enough to command overall confidence within society is government, it has fallen to government to fulfill the role nowadays of producer and guarantor of currency. The overwhelming collective need within any advanced economy for a functioning currency dictates that this is so; yet this role is neither unnatural for nor unwelcome to government, because being the largest entity in an economy puts government in the position of also having the greatest individual interest – of all entities within the economy – in creating and maintaining a stable currency there.

Bearing in mind the fundamental importance of confidence here, a government's policy relating to its currency should be oriented strictly around the nurturing of such confidence. This means that sound monetary and fiscal policies should be followed, and that a stance of complete transparency should be adopted so that such soundness of policy can be clearly seen. Moreover, considering that the value of transparency is diluted to any degree that simplicity is lost from the process, the monetary and fiscal policies to be followed not only should be sound, but they should be uncomplicated as well. The lack of such simplicity is the main problem with current monetary policy, and the primary reason for such lack is the dependence on central bank lending to regulate the money supply.

How does central bank lending complicate currency management? It introduces a middleman into the process of injecting currency into the economy. The presence of this middleman (group of middlemen) causes a rise in complexity because where there had been one locus of will here (the government), now there is that one plus as many more as there are independent middlemen. This increases the guesswork involved in managing the money supply of any fair-sized economy. Furthermore, the mere existence of a middleman layer necessitates mechanisms facilitating its incorporation into the process, the result being entrenched complication.

So how can we remove central bank lending from currency management and still regulate the money supply smoothly? By using government spending to keep the desired amount of cash in the money supply day by day so that the overall cash flow of the currency remains steady at all times. This "macro-cash flow" must be our primary focus here, and the perpetual maintenance of its stability our goal. What, essentially, is "macro-cash flow"? "Macro-cash flow" is the ongoing expression of will within a currency; it is the aggregate of the millions and millions of transactions occurring each day in that currency, every single transaction representing a unique exertion of will. Government, being the largest single participant in the economy, and overwhelmingly so, necessarily has a greater effect on macro-cash flow than anyone else. It is this capacity that we must harness to our purpose. Modern technology will assist us in this.

The full digitization of currency has not yet occurred. We still have coins and paper bills. However, such digitization is now just around the corner. Once it is complete we will very easily be able to monitor macro-cash flow on a daily basis. This will enable us to create a macro-cash flow index whose purpose is to indicate on any given day the precise amount of time, to the nanosecond, the average dollar sits idle between transactions. To regulate macro-cash flow, it is government's rate of discretionary spending, its discretionary infusion of cash into the money supply, that must be metered because neither non-discretionary spending nor taxation, on the revenue side, is amenable to such metering. This is a limitation, but considering the extent of governmental discretionary spending, not significantly so. The macro-cash flow index will be the basis on which the government meters its rate of discretionary spending, and thus regulates the money supply smoothly.

At first glance it may seem that this proposed system will allow for the ungoverned printing (creation) of money, a very dangerous thing. The truth is precisely the opposite. While money will continually be created in tandem with the expansion of the economy, thus addressing the need for the equivalent expansion of the money supply, such creation of money will be regulated very precisely to fill the shortfall between non-discretionary government spending and the total desired infusion of cash into the money supply on any given day. Moreover, this creation of money will be readily quantifiable, thus allowing for a simple and straightforward accounting of it to the general public updated on an ongoing basis day by day. Members of the public will be able to see that these figures match the currency needs as indicated by the macro-cash flow index. Such transparency, reinforced by the underlying simplicity of quantification, can only serve to strengthen confidence in the currency.

Although macro-cash flow, rather than inflation per se, is the focus of this proposal, the tendency here will be to produce an inflation-neutral money supply. The only factor that will counter this is macro-cash flow efficiency gains. A hundred years ago the average dollar sat idle between transactions far longer than the average dollar does today, and this efficiency gain can be expected to continue on into the foreseeable future. To keep from allowing this factor to contribute to inflation, an inflation index can be used to detect such gains and periodic adjustments can then be made to balance them out.

Many details will be necessary for fine-tuning the proposed system. For instance, if currency manipulation via repetitive transactions arises then it can easily be countered through the imposition of a minuscule transaction tax. However, systemic simplicity should be maintained to as great a degree as possible.

Confidence is the foundation of any currency. Modern technology is giving us the tools now not only to quantify and monitor such confidence on a daily basis but also to compensate for all the fluctuations in it so as to maintain our currency in a state of perfect stability. By adopting the proposed system based on the macro-cash flow index, we can best harness technological advance to accomplish this objective.

CO-OPRENISM

A corporation is the entitized expression of will. As such, both the formulation and the exertion of will are essential for its successful establishment. If there were a simple role delineation between the two then we could say that the entrepreneurs provide the formulation of will and the employees its exertion. However, not only do some corporations start out small enough that their entrepreneurs are also their sole initial providers of labor, but even those that are larger than that to begin with require some degree of formulation of will on the part of their employees as they pursue the visions of the entrepreneurs. Nevertheless, the roles of entrepreneur and employee are distinct enough from each other that the corporation is understood best when we differentiate between the two in this way.

In addition to the roles of entrepreneur and employee, establishment of the typical corporation requires a third element and that is capital. Capital is the past expression of will – past enterprise – that has been reduced [normally] to the liquid form of money. In relation to the corporation it also represents the present expression of will any time there is a transfer of funds from the investor to the corporation, that at start-up being pertinent here. The form that this expression of will takes is confidence – the development and concrete expression of trust – in the entrepreneur, in the entrepreneur's vision and ability to deliver, on the part of the investor. So the corporation is the entitized expression of will and there are three essential roles in the establishment of the typical corporation: entrepreneur, employee and investor.

What should be the relationship of these three elements of the corporation to the corporation itself as embodied in its ownership structure? It is common today for such ownership to be split between the entrepreneurs and investors. It is also fairly common for corporations to use stock options and other means to encourage or assist their employees to acquire company shares. However, employee ownership of corporations very seldom reaches the level where any real measure of fundamental control passes into the hands of the employees per se. So the typical corporation is owned mainly by its entrepreneurs and investors and controlled by the same to the exclusion of its employees.

There is a serious problem with excluding employees from the fundamental control of the corporations they work for, and that is that doing so dehumanizes their labor. Ask any small business owner his reasons for owning his own business and, "Being my own boss," will likely be his first response. That expresses his reaction against the inherent dehumanization that laboring under the command of others entails. No amount of remuneration can change this. The ability to resign from one's position of employment, to leave one job and find another, keeps such dehumanization from reaching the totalitarian level attained in outright slavery, but this is only the amelioration of an inequity and not its removal. The labor of employees who are excluded from the fundamental control of the corporations they work for is inherently dehumanized, and this dehumanization has as negative an impact on these corporations as it does on their employees. One consequence of such dehumanization is that the bond the employees feel toward their corporations is considerably weakened, resulting in the sort of productivity losses that come from the lack – or lessening – of worker conscientiousness and concern for corporate interests. Another, and even more dire, consequence of such dehumanization is the subsequent loss by the corporation of full access to the most powerful tool any worker can bring to the table: his own mind. Whether it is due to his increased confidence in the legitimacy of his actions or to his heightened sense of urgency in carrying out his responsibilities, ownership and control of his own business allows for the full engagement of the business owner's mind in furthering his enterprise – this in contrast to labor performed under the command of another where the mental output of the worker is necessarily and naturally narrowed in scope to that minuscule portion of the spectrum which is adequate for the successful performance of such labor.

Through their growing recognition of the importance of worker
empowerment, it is beginning to dawn on the corporate world
how powerful the human mind can be. In response to this new
awareness, many corporations have developed policies and
mechanisms that seek to address the matter, things like job
rotation, job enlargement, employee feedback, flex time and
incentive programs. Such things are beneficial in their limited
way; nevertheless they are ultimately little more than window
dressing because they address the problem only at a superficial
level and not at its root. The issue here is control, the fact that the
full potential of the immensely powerful tool that is the human
mind can be realized only when that tool is fully under its own
control – or, at least, so perceives itself to be. This means, in the
context of the corporation, that only those minds that have a
meaningful share of its fundamental control – a meaningful share
in its ownership structure – will have any chance of becoming
fully engaged in its service on a genuine and sustainable basis.
So the standard ownership structure of corporations today is
more than adequate in engaging the minds of entrepreneurs – and
investors, for that matter, in their more limited role focused on
assessing the entrepreneurs' visions and abilities to deliver on
the same – but woefully inadequate in doing the same with the
minds of employees. The challenge is to come up with a
reformed ownership structure that brings employees, the minds
of employees, into the mix here on a similarly meaningful basis.
The reward will be the realization of a whole new type of

corporation which not only is more robust than that in existence today but also makes a more positive overall contribution to society and the common welfare.

The issue of control is so simple, yet at the same time so complex. Here we have just three entities, three groups to split the pie between: investors, entrepreneurs and employees. How difficult could it be to arrive at an acceptable division? How difficult indeed!

Let it be clear that the objective is to raise employee ownership and control of the corporation from its present near-nothing to that of eventual equal stakeholder. This is a dramatic restructuring. Is it justified? Yes. The employees in the typical corporation today greatly outnumber its entrepreneurs and investors combined. This means that the available mind power currently not being fully accessed well exceeds that which is being fully accessed. Seen in this light, in light of the human mind and its potential, raising employees collectively to the status of equal stakeholder in the corporation is a justified and desirable outcome, and this for entrepreneurs and investors every bit as much as for employees. What degree of ownership and control that is lost thus by entrepreneurs and investors will be more than compensated for by the subsequent increased robustness, vitality and profitability of their corporations.

Toward the end of reforming the corporate ownership structure as described, the following model is proposed. In it the corporation makes the transition from a preliminary stage of ownership and control into its fully matured state; this is necessary because at the corporation's inception there are no employees or, if there are some, their commitment and value to the corporation remain unknown. In both its preliminary stage and mature state, 50% of all classes of shares in the corporation will be held as a single bloc by a trust (the "co-opreneur trust") representing and democratically controlled by the employees and entrepreneurs collectively. The other 50% will be split between the investors and entrepreneurs per negotiation but with the standard division being 35% going to the investors and the remaining 15% going to the entrepreneurs. Although the actual division of shares will not change from the preliminary stage to the mature state, in the preliminary stage the entrepreneurs will have sole control of the co-opreneur trust and its bloc of shares by default, whereas such control will be in the hands of the employees in the mature state.

The co-opreneur trust is the linchpin of the proposed model. It is reasonable that anyone being raised to "co-opreneur" status first work with the corporation for some minimum period of time so that their commitment to and fit within the company can be evaluated fully. It is also reasonable to expect the attainment by prospective co-opreneurs of certain defined skills and knowledge, whether general or specific, as the case may be. These factors necessarily delay expansion of the "co-opreneurship" beyond the group of entrepreneurs for some time following the corporation's establishment. Such expansion, the election of employees to co-opreneur status, is decided upon by the existing co-opreneurs and specifically requires their majority approval. This being the case, it becomes clear that the important threshold representing the transition from the corporation's preliminary stage to its mature state (in the structural sense with no reference to the attainment of profitability or other critical milestones) is reached when the number of co-opreneurs is more than double the number of entrepreneurs, so that the entrepreneurs no longer control the co-opreneur trust; instead, such control has now been ceded to the employees, collectively, and with it considerable control over the corporation as a whole.

Achieving this structural maturity is an important, yet also a momentous, step. It is understandable that both investors and entrepreneurs view it with a certain amount of trepidation. They, who have made significant tangible investments in the corporation, are about to entrust it to the employees, a group of people whose investment in it will come in the future, and will even then be mostly intangible. To address this trepidation, certain safeguards can be built into the structures of both the corporation and the co-opreneur trust. Issues such as salaries, co-opreneur election (and ejection), dividend payments and the liquidation of the corporation in the event of bankruptcy, to name only a few, should be dealt with in this way.

This proposed corporate ownership structure is neither utopian nor an exercise in altruism. It is simply good business, teamwork-oriented good business that recognizes what a powerful tool the human mind is. It sees the corporation as a collection of minds more than anything else. Structuring the corporation so as to place its control in the hands of those whose minds comprise it, from the janitors to the executives and everyone in between, is the only way to overcome the costly dehumanization of their labor that is otherwise inevitable; moreover, it is the best way to impart authenticity to the worthy pursuit of worker empowerment.

MEANS

There is nothing earth-shatteringly original about the ideas I
have expressed. Threads of them are to be found woven all
throughout the fabric of society and the larger reality. Neither is
there anything particularly original about my formula for their
implementation: discipline, patience and hard work... and
patience... and more patience... and more patience.

Our challenge is to bring about certain adjustments to ourselves,
our lifestyles, our societies and humanity as a whole so as to
realize our complete alignment according to the compass of
bioism. This is not an easy task. It will not be completed in a
generation. It may not be completed in ten generations. Where
do we begin? Some might see the control of government, that
fundamental tool in the guidance and direction of society, as a
primary objective and predicate the formation of a party as a
logical first step. While I would not rule out such a strategy as
that, I am personally inclined to see these ideas as far too
ecumenical to be contained within a single party. In fact, my
perception of these ideas is that they are every bit as much the
foundation of the left-wing as of the right, not to mention
countless other perspectives outside the left/right paradigm.
Rather than seeing a need for new vehicles, new organizations,

for the successful implementation of these ideas, I would encourage their percolation throughout all existing vehicles, be they parties, governments, religious institutions, educational institutions or other organizations that have an influence on society. In such a context it would then be immensely effective for like-minded individuals to coalesce into loose associations (within organizations) the better to promote and implement shared ideas. At the same time we must always remember that an individual's first responsibility is over himself: Extending the implementation of these ideas on an ever-widening scale is a constantly valid objective; however, there will be frequent failures and setbacks in this respect, and these should never be allowed to undermine one's own course and resolve on the individual level. In this way we can be confident of long-term success in spite of all the inevitable potholes in the road along the way.

As to tactics, we must have a definite preference for, and orientation towards, taking the high road. Reason is on our side. The use of offensive force or underhanded means, as opposed to reason, is a sign of weakness. More than anything else it is our thought that makes us strong, the strongest of all. This is not to suggest that violence should be combated with passivity, or deviousness with naiveté; however, any time we find ourselves resorting to the anti-rational means of force or deception, we must inspect ourselves and our motives stringently to be sure our actions are justified responses to the same rather than opportunistic initiatives on our own part breaded with justification. To do less would be a betrayal of ourselves, a betrayal of our ideals and a betrayal of biosity itself, of which we are the arch-stewards. People talk about the end justifying the means, but this overlooks the fact that today's end is tomorrow's means. "That which a man sows, so also shall he reap." Life is a continuum of means.

GARY WILSON

Request for Review

Thank you for reading *BIOISM: The Deity of Life*. It has been a privilege for me to share my thoughts with you in this way. If you have enjoyed – or are still enjoying – this work, I would be grateful and delighted if you would write a quick review of it. To do so please log in to Amazon, find *BIOISM: The Deity of Life,* click on the *customer reviews* link and then click on the *Write a customer review* link.

Thank you for considering this, Gary

Works by Gary Wilson

Island (the one that wasn't supposed to be)

Gary's first novel, this story follows a young man overtaken by
events who finds himself a fugitive fleeing from the law.
Although a tale of action, it is in the interludes of thought that we
see that this narrative serves as an analysis and criticism of
existentialism. See sample chapter below.

Where Then O Bliss

A prequel to *Island (the one that wasn't supposed to be)*, this
romance about the love between an idealistic student and a
victim of severe spousal abuse serves as an analysis and criticism
of romanticism. See sample chapter below.

Bioism: The Deity of Life

A compilation of essays elucidating the philosophy that Gary has
developed, bioism. See sample essay, *The Age of Sophistry*,
below.

Relativity Riddled: Inframotionality

A physics model that is an alternative to the standard physics model and overcomes the structural defects of relativity. See excerpt below.

Please visit www.garywilson.ca to see more details and the most current listing of the works by Gary Wilson.

About the Author

Gary Wilson is a Canadian, born and raised in Calgary. His life has been varied, exposing him to considerably more than many people ever experience. After spending his 20's searching for meaning in life, he was accepted into law school in Houston due to his high ranking on the LSAT. Shortly thereafter he was charged with homicide and spent a year on the run in a myriad of lifestyles before turning himself in. His 30's were spent locked up and in contact with people of many backgrounds and ethnicities. It was during this time of concentrated and undistracted thought that Gary formulated the ideas resulting in bioism. Today he lives with his wife and children in Calgary where he is a business owner.

Island (the one that wasn't supposed to be) [Excerpt]

Chapter 2

My name is, say, Barry. No, really, that is my name. Barry. Barry, uuuh, Klassen. I guess I'm a little ambiguous on this point because the driver's license in my pocket has a different name on it. I can't recall that name at this precise moment—which is bad, very foolish, very careless of me. It's always important to know your name. You never know when you may need to say it. "Hello, Officer Friendly, my name is uuuh... I mean... uuuh Barry? No, no, no, uuuh Kerry—yeah, Kerry Coddington." That, dear Reader, is not a successful verbal transaction. Officer Friendly, who otherwise is useful for directions and even, in dire circumstances (as I learned six months ago almost to the day), aid, will not respond well to such clumsiness. Happily, I can say that I have never actually fumbled quite so badly as that—though often, with so many names on God's green earth to choose from, it has only been my iron will that has kept me focused, that has kept me from dawdling too long in that name-shopper's paradise, whenever there has been a present at hand needing my full attention. (However, one time at work I did answer the phone

217

and say, "This is Gary, I mean, Cary..." That was not adept. The coworker on the other end of the line did not matter per se, but in a spirit of discretion I very soon left that employ).

Discretion: that is the key to traveling. I like this word, "traveling." And I endorse it as descriptive of what I am doing right now (in the extended present "right now," as opposed to the ahorita kind of "right now"), what I have been doing for the last 10 months. I really do not appreciate people, like my lawyer, with their faux criminal subculture "on the lam." I do not have tattoos. I am not opportunistically eyeing every passing 7/11 for a shot at an easy $30 and change. And I do not slink through alleys looking for a fight. (Besides all that, I have yet to be arrested—so there! Case closed!) If you want to be so unnecessary with words as to say that I am traveling incognito, I could roll my eyes and say, "Sure. Fine. Alright. Whatever!" But, truth to tell, I am not even incognito. Many people have known me this past year, and known me well. The name that I received at birth is just one part of me and has proven, time and time again, to be beside the point in my interactions with others. When you go to Safeway and buy a loaf of bread, do you tell the cashier your name? Or do you care if her name "really" is Joyce, as her name-tag says, or if it "actually" is Jill? And just because her parents christened her with some verbal identifier like "Joyce," or "Jill" now, should we really be so primitive as to attach any deeper significance to the matter than simple convenience? So, in all honesty, I am simply traveling—and I am really enjoying my travels. There is nothing like a nation-wide arrest warrant hanging over your head to add a little spice to life, to keep you on your toes and teach you the existential responsibility of genuine discretion. (Whoever—my first guess would have to be that swashbuckler John Calvin—said that the life lived without intensity wasn't worth living, really hit the nail on the head.)

End of excerpt from **Island (the one that wasn't supposed to be).**

Where Then O Bliss [Excerpt]

Part One

Chapter 1

Where then, O bliss, is thy balm?
Where, O rapture, thine infinite?

Allen Bill Pond...

As the sun lies dying at Allen Bill Pond, thoughts of Felicia fill the recess of my mind.

Felicia of the unpronounceable last name. Felicia, Felicia, Felicia...

Actually, her name is Felicja, but it corresponds to Felicia in

English. Fay-lee-tsya in her native Poland, Fe-lee-sha over here.

I met Felicia early last year. We were both enrolled in an intensive course of environmental studies. Though we were part of a small group of twenty or so people attending long classes daily, we are both standoffish enough that it took us a few days to introduce ourselves to each other and become acquainted. By the time we did do so, it had already become as clear to her as it was to me that we were kindred spirits.

What is it that identifies a kindred spirit, Reader? As I sit here twirling my pen pondering this, the main thing that seems to stand out is intelligence — intelligence as seen in the eyes and the poise or bearing of a person, intelligence plus a little je ne sais quoi. At least, that's what comes to mind as I think of this in relation to Felicia. I don't recall any specific action or words on her part that revealed her to me any more clearly than did the intelligence and that special something I could see in her eyes and poise. I like to think too that the same applied in regard to her perception of me, but be that as it may. What I do know is that when Felicia saw me spending my time staring out the window rather than paying attention in class, she figured that she had found a kindred spirit; and when she heard me introduce myself to the class by saying my name, pausing, wrinkling my brow and then slowly continuing with, "I can think of all kinds of things about myself that I don't want to tell you, but I'm having trouble coming up with anything I do want to tell you," she knew that she'd found one.

Felicia is beautiful. This is true and necessary, necessary twice over. First, this is a story I'm writing. Never mind the fact that it might be perceived by some as a true story. It is still a story, and in our culture the female lead in a story, be it a book, movie or whatever else, is beautiful. It's one of the failings of our culture. And secondly, I myself incarnate this same weakness such that I'm able to love only beautiful women. Try as I might, and believe me I have tried hard, I am completely unable to arouse any passion within myself for the plain-Janes of this world, no matter that they are often the more beautiful in spirit.

That said, let me tell you, Reader, how beautiful Felicia is. She once told me that Polish girls in general are beautiful. I believe her. I have no reason to disbelieve her. Felicia is slender and of medium height. I never saw her with dark hair, even though that's her natural color. Always when I knew her she was blonde, sometimes a straw-blonde and sometimes with a hint of henna. The color of one's hair by no means determines or even enhances beauty, but when Felicia's visiting mother-in-law was pressuring her to go back to brunette, I thwarted the matron's efforts with a single disparaging remark — merely because I did not want my beautiful girl to change in any way.

Felicia's eyes are the color of the Seine, a soft and serene brown lightened with flecks of green. I've enjoyed many, many hours diving into those waters, basking in the subtlety of the main current, being tickled by the tug of innumerable undercurrents. I dare say no more — dare think no more — of Felicia's eyes.

Although a picture says a thousand words, the reverse is not true: A thousand words do not say a picture. This is a pity because it makes it difficult for me to help you envision Felicia. When she was without a speck of make-up, I found her beautiful in a very Slavic way. I would mention full lips, wide spacing of eyes and prominent cheekbones, for whatever illumination that might cast. Made up, she looks very Euro, very enchantress-mystery-of-kohl; she is the fin-de-siècle answer to, image of, Brigitte Bardot.

Is Felicia a smiler, a sunny personality? Need you ask, Reader?

I knew Felicia to smile but seldom. Her smiles were like gems, rare and precious. I think — rather, I should say that I know — that this was something that drew her to me. I am confused within myself as to what I mean by this: On the one hand, it is true that she perceived me, as it seems does everyone, to be as austere in countenance as I have just described her. She once saw some old photos of me in which I had long blond hair and I was just staring existentially at the camera. She was struck by these photos. She saw herself in them. And she was right. It might as well have been her staring at the camera, thinly disguised, very thinly disguised, by my features. But on the other hand, appearances can be, and in this case are, deceiving, for I am a veritable well of optimism and inner sanguinity. Unlike Felicia, whose solemnity of demeanor is due to a profound sadness, my own is more akin to ennui. So I'm not entirely unconfused as to whether she was drawn to a bird of her own feather, or attracted to an opposite. I suspect that, paradoxically, both are true.

Let me get Jean-Paul and France out of the way right now. No conscious attempt has been made to season the preceding passages along such lines. The simple fact is that Felicia is a true Pole and the heart of every true Pole lives in Paris no matter whether the body resides there too or in Chicago, London or Warsaw itself. For me to think or talk about Felicia completely without reference to things French would be both nonsensical and impossible; it would be like talking about Catherine the Great with no mention of Russia, Cleopatra without Rome, Helen sans Troy — simply preposterous.

Have I given you a fair enough picture of Felicia yet? Are you able to visualize an image that is more personality than anonymity? Can you begin to comprehend her beauty? Now let me tell you the anomaly: Felicia wears glasses. We all know from Hollywood's teaching that a beautiful girl need do nothing more strenuous than donning a pair of glasses to turn herself into a frump, a wallflower ignored by all men. (Didn't Marilyn Monroe, of all people, do this precise thing in one or more of her movies?) And of course we also know what baloney that is, for various reasons. Well, interestingly enough, in Felicia's case this "wallflower effect" is very nearly fully realized. This is because of her lens prescription. When nearsighted people wear glasses, others do not see their eyes to appear magnified; in fact, the opposite is true, but it is only with strong lenses that the eyes appear noticeably shrunken. It is farsighted people who wear glasses that make their eyes appear magnified ("googly-eyed", to use the scientific term); but since most farsighted people wear glasses only while reading (or not at all, for that matter), it's really a small percentage of regular glasses-wearers whose appearance is actually changed very drastically by the donning of glasses. It just so happens, though, that Felicia is one of these.

She is farsighted, and worse yet (in this respect), farsighted in only one eye. When she was a child growing up in Poland, she had a severe bout with one of the childhood diseases. Due to the lack there at the time of the appropriate medication, she almost lost her young life, but ended up pulling through. This affliction left its mark on her, though, in the form of a scarred retina in one eye. Imagine, then, our Felicia having just put on her glasses as described. It really does not matter, does it, how beautiful she is? She has effectively concealed her beauty and transformed herself into the proverbial wallflower.

End of excerpt from **Where Then O Bliss.**

Introduction [excerpted from Relativity Riddled: Inframotionality]

Relativity has problems. The biggest problem of all is that acknowledgement and discussion of these problems is taboo. No one in the physics community today countenances skepticism of relativity, much less harbors it. On the one hand, this community insists that it alone is competent to analyze and evaluate relativity; and on the other hand, it insists on the full, unthinking embrace of relativity – even, and especially, within itself. So where is left any forum for a scientific skepticism of relativity?

If the physics community's state of denial were relativity's only problem then it wouldn't be much of a problem. But it's not. Relativity has fundamental inadequacies. These will be examined in the following presentation of an alternative physics model, the Inframotionality Model.

End of excerpt from **Relativity Riddled: Inframotionality.**

www.ingramcontent.com/pod-product-compliance
Lightning Source LLC
Chambersburg PA
CBHW020405150626
46554CB00012B/274